First studies of plant life

George Francis Atkinson

Alpha Editions

This edition published in 2019

ISBN : 9789353864767

Design and Setting By
Alpha Editions
email - alphaedis@gmail.com

FIRST STUDIES OF
PLANT LIFE

BY

GEORGE FRANCIS ATKINSON, Ph.B.

PROFESSOR OF BOTANY IN CORNELL UNIVERSITY

BOSTON, U.S.A.

GINN & COMPANY, PUBLISHERS

The Athenæum Press

1902

INTRODUCTION

For a long time botanical science, in the popular mind, consisted chiefly of pulling flowers to pieces and finding their Latin names by the use of the analytical key. All the careful descriptions of the habits of plants in the classic books were viewed solely as conducive to accuracy in placing the proper label upon herbarium specimens. Long after the study of botany in the universities had become biological rather than purely systematic, the old régime held sway in our secondary schools; and perhaps some of us to-day know of high schools still working in the twilight of that first ray that pierced primeval darkness. However, this has practically passed away, and to-day life and its problems, its successes and its failures, absorb the attention of the botanist and zoölogist. The knowledge of the name of the plant or animal is simply a convenience for discrimination and reference. The systematic relations of a plant or animal are used in showing present anatomical affinities and past development. The absorbing themes of investigation and study are the life processes and the means by which the organisms living in the world to-day have climbed upward and placed themselves in the great realm of the "fit."

When the idea of nature study first dawned in the educational world, it was inevitably confused with the sciences on which it was based. Hence in earlier times we tried to teach the nature study of plants by making the children pull the flowers to pieces and learn the names of their different parts. This was as bad nature study as it was bad science, for we were violating the laws of the child's nature. The child cares very little about the forms of things; he is far more interested in what things do.

To-day nature study and science, while they may deal with the same objects, view them from opposite standpoints. Nature study is not synthetic; it takes for its central thought the child, and for its field work the child's natural environment. The child, through nature study, learns to know the life history of the violet growing in his own dooryard, and the fascinating story of the robin nesting in the cornice of his own porch. The differences of this violet and this robin from other violets and other robins in the world he considers not at all.

That the plant as well as the animal in nature study should be regarded a thing of life has long been recognized, and most of our nature study of plants begins with the planting and sprouting of the seed. Unfortunately, it mostly stops here; the life processes of the plant have seemed too complex to be brought within the comprehension of the child. There is much of chemistry in operations of plant growth, and we find very few things in chemistry that are simple enough to be properly a part of nature study.

"First Studies of Plant Life" has been written with the sole view of bringing the life processes of the plant within the reach of the child and, with the aid of the competent teacher, it will certainly be comprehensible to the pupil of even the lower grades. In this book the plant stands before the child as a living being with needs like his own. To live, the plant must be born, must be nourished, must breathe, must reproduce, and, after experiencing these things, must die. Each plant that is grown in the window box of a schoolroom should reveal to the child the secrets and the story of a whole life. He realizes that the young plant must be fed; it must grow; it is no longer a matter of commonplace; it is replete with interest, because it is the struggle of an individual to live. How does it get its food? How does it grow? It is of little moment whether its leaves are lanceolate or palmate; it is a question of what the leaves do for the plant; it is a matter of life or death.

When the child has once become acquainted with the conditions and necessities of plant life, how different will the world seem to him! Every glance at forest or field will tell him a new story. Every square foot of sod will be revealed to him as a battlefield in which he himself may count the victories in the struggle for existence, and he will walk henceforward in a world of miracle and of beauty, — the miracle of adjustment to circumstances, and the beauty of obedience to law.　　　ANNA BOTSFORD COMSTOCK.

BUREAU OF NATURE STUDY,
CORNELL UNIVERSITY.

AUTHOR'S PREFACE

IN presenting these "First Studies of Plant Life" the object has been to interest the child and pupil in the life and work of plants. The child, or young pupil, is primarily interested in life or something real and active, full of action, of play, or play-work. Things which are in action, which represent states of action, or which can be used by the child in imitating or "staging" various activities or realities, are those which appeal most directly to him and which are most forceful in impressing on his mind the fundamental things on which his sympathies or interests can be built up.

There is, perhaps, a too general feeling that young pupils should be taught things; that the time for reasoning out why a thing is so, or why it behaves as it does under certain conditions, belongs to a later period of life. We are apt to forget that during the first years of his existence the child is dependent largely on his own resources, his own activity of body and mind, in acquiring knowledge. He is preëminently an investigator, occupied with marvelous observations and explorations of his environment.

Why then should we not encourage a continuance of this kind of knowledge-seeking on the part of the child? The young pupil cannot, of course, be left entirely to himself in working out the relation and meaning of things. But opportunities often present themselves when the child should be encouraged to make the observations and from these learn why the result is so. No more excellent opportunities are afforded than in nature study. The topics most suitable are those which deal with the life, or work, or the conditions and states of formation.

To the child or young pupil a story, or the materials from which a story can be constructed, is not only the most engaging theme, but offers the best opportunity for constructive thought and proper interpretation.

In the studies on the work of plants some of the topics will have to be presented entirely by the teacher, and will serve as reference matter for the pupil, as will all of the book on occasions. The chapter dealing with the chemical changes in the work of starch-making is recognized by the author as dealing with too technical a subject for young pupils, and is included chiefly to round out the part on the work of plants. Still it involves no difficult reasoning, and if young children can appreciate, as many of them do, the "Fairyland of Chemistry," the pupils may be able to get at least a general notion of what is involved in the changes outlined in this chapter.

The chapters on Life Stories of Plants the author has attempted to present in the form of biographies. They suggest that biographies are to be read from the plants themselves by the pupils. In fact, this feature of reading the stories which plants have to tell forms the leading theme which runs through the book. The plants talk by a "sign language," which the pupil is encouraged to read and interpret. This method lends itself in a happy manner as an appeal to the child's power of interpretation of the things which it sees.

Many older persons will, perhaps, be interested in some of these stories, especially in the Struggles of a White Pine.

The story on the companionship of plants also affords a topic of real interest to the pupil, suggesting social conditions and relations of plants which can be read and interpreted by the young. Nearly all of the line drawings are original, and were made expressly for this book by Mr. Frank R. Rathbun, Auburn, N.Y. Figs. 64, 79, 215, 216, 260 were reproduced from Bergen's "Botany," and Fig. 84, from Circular 86, United States Department of Agriculture, by Mr. Chesnut. The author desires to acknowledge his indebtedness to the following persons, who have kindly contributed photographs : Mr. H. E. Murdock, for the Frontispiece ; Prof. Conway Mac-Millan, University of Minnesota, for Figs. 220, 249, 257 ; Professor Gifford, Cornell University, for Figs. 87, 183, 285, 290, 293, 295 ; Mr. Gifford Pinchot, Division of Forestry, United States Department of Agriculture, for Figs. 280, 282, 289, 292 ; Prof. W. W. Rowlee, Cornell University, for Figs. 279, 281, 304 ; Miss A. V. Luther, for Figs. 200, 296, 302; Prof. P. H. Mell, for Fig. 278 ; Prof. William Trelease, Missouri Botanical Garden, for Fig. 307 ; Professor Tuomey, Yale University, for Fig. 306. Fig. 221 is reproduced from photographs by Mr. K. Miyake ; Fig. 77, from photograph by Mr. H. Hasselbring ; Figs. 76, 288, from photographs by Dr. W. A. Murrill. The remaining photographs were made by the author. Some of the text-figures were reproduced from the author's "Elementary Botany," while the photographs of mushrooms are from some of those published in Bulletins 138 and 168 of the Cornell University Agricultural Experiment Station, and from the author's "Mushrooms, Edible, Poisonous, etc."

GEO. F. ATKINSON.

CORNELL UNIVERSITY, March, 1901.

CONTENTS

xi

PART III: THE BEHAVIOR OF PLANTS

PART IV: LIFE STORIES OF PLANTS

PART V: BATTLES OF PLANTS IN THE WORLD

FIRST STUDIES OF PLANT LIFE

PART I

THE GROWTH AND PARTS OF PLANTS

CHAPTER I

HOW SEEDLINGS COME UP FROM THE GROUND

The life in a dry seed. For this study we shall use seeds of beans, peas, corn, pumpkin, sunflower, and buckwheat. You may use some other seeds if they are more convenient, but these are easy to get at feed stores or seed stores. If you did not know that they were seeds of plants, you would not believe that these dry and hard objects had any life in them. They show no signs of life while they are kept for weeks or months in the packet or bag in a dry room.

But plant the seeds in damp soil in the garden or field during the warm season, or plant them in a box or pot of damp soil kept in a warm room. For several days there is no sign that any change is taking place in the seeds. But in a few days or a week, if it is not too cold, some of the surface earth above the

buried seeds is disturbed, lifted, or cracked. Rising through this opening in the surface soil there is a young green plant. We see that it has life now, because it grows and has the power to push its way through the soil. The dry seed was alive, but could not grow. The plant life was dormant in the dry seed. What made the plant life active when the seed was buried in the soil?

FIG. 1. Bean seedlings breaking through the soil.

How the corn seedling gets out of the ground. One should watch for the earliest appearance of the seedlings coming through the soil. The corn seedling seems to come up with little difficulty. It comes up straight, as a slender, pointed object which pierces through the soil easily, unless the earth is very hard, or a clod or stone lies above the seedling. It looks like a tender stem, but in a few days more it unrolls, or unwinds, and long, slender leaves appear, so that what

FIG. 2. Corn seedlings coming up.

we took for a stem was not a stem at all, but delicate leaves wrapped round each other so tightly as to push their way through the soil unharmed. What would have happened to the leaves if they had unfolded in the ground?

How the bean behaves in coming out of the ground. When we look for the bean seedling as it is coming

up we see that the stem is bent into a loop. This loop forces its way through the soil, dragging on one end the bean that was buried. Sometimes the outer coat of the seed clings to the bean as it comes from the ground, but usually this slips off and

FIG. 3. The "loop" of the bean seedling.

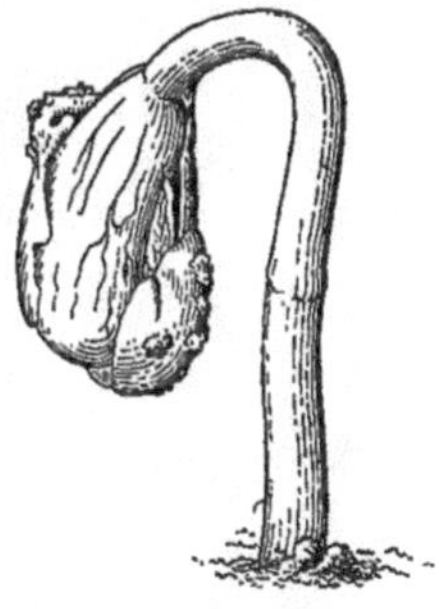

is left in the ground. Soon after the loop appears above ground it straightens out and lifts the bean several inches high. As the bean is being raised above ground the outer coat slips off. Now we see that the bean is split into two thick parts (*cot-y-le'dons*), which spread farther and farther apart, showing between them young green leaves, which soon expand into well-formed bean leaves.

The pea seedling comes up in a different way. The stem of the pea also comes up in a loop. As it

FIG. 4. Germinating bean shedding the seed coats.

straightens up we look in vain for the pea on the end. There are small green leaves, but no thick part of the pea which was buried in the ground. This part of the

pea, then, must have been left in the ground. When
we have seen how the other seedlings come up, we
can plant more seeds in such a
way as to see just how each seed
germinates, and learn the reason
for the different behavior of the
seedlings in coming from
the ground.

**The pumpkin seedling
also comes up in a loop,**
and on one end of the
loop, as it is
being lifted
through the
soil, we see
two flat,
rather thick
parts. To-

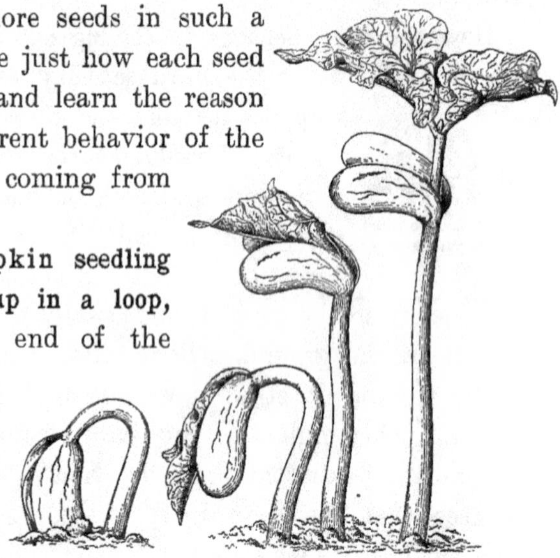

Fig. 5.   Bean seedlings straightening up; the plumule and
spreading leaves showing from between the cotyledons.

gether they are about the size of the pumpkin seed.
By looking carefully we may sometimes find the old
shell, or seed coat, still clinging to the tips
of these parts of the seed ; the shell is split
part way down only, and so pinches tightly
over the tips.   Usually, however, it is left
empty in the ground.

Fig. 6. Pea seed-
lings coming up.

It will be interesting later to see how
this little pumpkin plant gets out of its shell.   It

usually escapes while still buried in the soil.
As the loop straightens out, these two thick
portions spread wide apart in the light and
become green.

There are little lines
on them resembling
the "veins" on some
leaves. Are these
two parts of the

FIG. 7. Pumpkin seedlings coming from the ground,
showing loop and opening cotyledons.

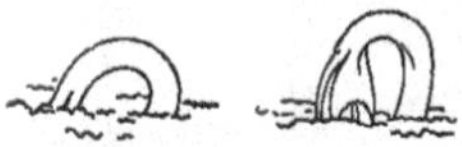

pumpkin seed real leaves? Look down between them
where they join the stem. Very young leaves are
growing out from between them.

The sunflower seedling. The sunflower seedling comes up with a loop,
dragging the seed
on one end. The

FIG. 8. Loop on stem of
sunflower as it comes
from the ground.

shell, or seed coat, is sometimes left
in the ground, because it splits farther
through when the root wedges its way
out. But often the seed coat
clings to the tips of the cotyledons until the plant straightens. Then the cotyledons
usually spread far apart. The
seed coat of the pumpkin
sometimes clings to the tips

FIG. 9. Seedlings of sunflower casting
seed coats as cotyledons open.

of the cotyledons until the sunlight pries them apart.

The buckwheat seedling. This also comes up with a loop, and we begin to see that this way of coming up is very common among seedlings. The seed coat of the buckwheat is often lifted above ground on one end of the loop. It is split nearly across. Through the split in the seed we can see that there are leaves packed inside very differently from the way in which the cotyledons of

FIG. 10. Loop of buckwheat seedlings coming through the surface of the soil.

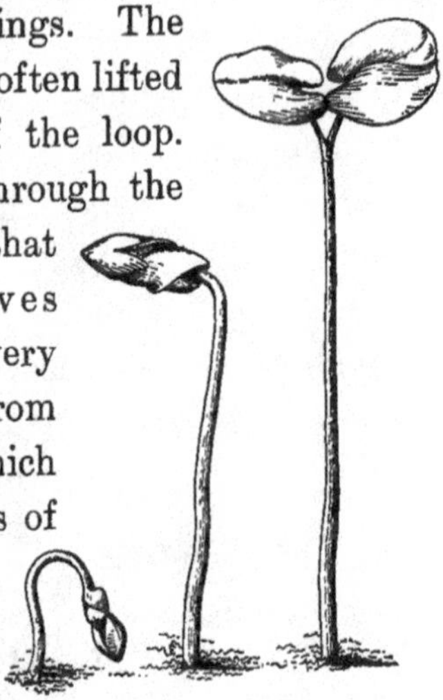

the pumpkin and sunflower lie. The buckwheat cotyledons are twisted or rolled round each other. As the seedling straightens up they untwist, and in doing this help to throw off the coat.

FIG. 11. Cotyledons of buckwheat seedlings untwisting and casting seed coats.

CHAPTER II

HOW THE SEEDS BEHAVE WHEN GERMINATING

To prepare the seeds for observation. We could not see how the seeds planted in the ground behaved while they were germinating, for they were hidden from sight. To watch the behavior of the different kinds, the seeds are put where there is warmth and moisture under glass, or they are covered with damp paper or moss, which may be lifted at any time to see what is going on. They may be grown in tumblers, or in shallow vessels covered with glass, with wet moss or paper inside. The best way to plant them for easy observation is to put them in a lamp chimney filled with wet peat moss or sawdust, as shown in Fig. 12. Or a box may be made with glass doors on the side.

FIG. 12. Corn seedlings growing in lamp chimney.

This may be filled with wet moss or sawdust, the seeds put in place, and the door then closed. If desired, some soft manila paper may be placed on the moss or

7

FIG. 13. Pumpkin seedlings growing in lamp chimney.

sawdust, and the seed placed between this and the glass. If the lamp chimney is used, roll the paper into a tube smaller than the chimney and slip it in. Now put the peat moss inside, not very tight. The seeds may be started between the glass and paper, and with a blunt wire may be pushed into any position desired.

The seeds first absorb water and swell. Before the seeds are planted for this study they should be soaked from twelve to twenty-four hours in water. Then they may be placed in the germinator for observation. Look at the seeds in the water several times during the day, and see what changes take place in them. All of them become larger. After they have been in the water for a day, cut one, and also try to cut one of the dry seeds. The seeds that have been soaked in water are softer and larger than the dry seed. Why is this so ? It must

FIG. 14. Box with glass door on side for growing seedlings.

be that they have taken in water, or have absorbed
water, as we say. This has increased their size, made
them wet inside, and soft.

How the pea and bean seeds swell. The pea
and bean swell in a curious way, as can be seen
by looking at them at short intervals after they

FIG. 15. Bean have been placed in the water. The water is
seed before
soaking in taken in at first more rapidly by the coat
water. of the seed than by the other parts. The coat
becomes much wrinkled then, as
if it were too big for the seed.
First the wrinkles begin to appear
round one edge. Then they become more numerous, and extend
farther over the surface, until the
entire coat is strongly wrinkled,

FIG. 16. Bean seeds with coats
wrinkling as they soak in
water.

as shown in Fig. 16. This loosens the coat from the
bulk of the seed, and perhaps is one reason
why this coat slips off so easily while the
loop of the stem is pulling the inside of
the seed out of the ground. Finally the
inside parts swell as they take up water.

FIG. 17. Bean seed
after soaking in They fill out the coat again so that it is
water, larger, and
now smooth. smooth, as shown in Fig. 17.

The first sign of the seedling. In a very few days,
now that the seeds are thoroughly soaked with water,
the signs of life begin to appear. The root grows out

of the seed as a small, white, slender, pointed object. It comes from the same spot in every seed of one kind. In the sunflower, pumpkin, buckwheat, and corn it comes from the smaller end of the seed. In the

FIG. 18. Corn seeds germinating under glass, the left-hand seed upside down.

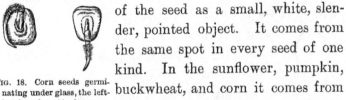

bean it comes out from the hollowed, or concave, side. As soon as the root comes out it grows directly downward, no matter which way the seed happens to lie.

When the seeds are placed in the lamp chimney, or in a box with a glass side, they can be easily held in any position desired. It will be interesting to watch seeds

FIG. 19.   Later stage of Fig. 18.

that have been placed in different positions. When the roots have grown an inch or more in length, sketch some of the different positions. Is there any advantage to the plant in having this first root grow downward?

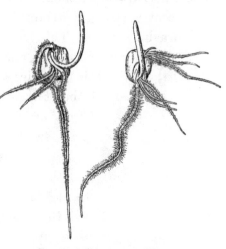

FIG. 20.   Still later stage of Fig. 18.

How the pumpkin plant gets out of the seed coat. As the root grows out of the small end of the seed, it acts like a wedge and often splits the shell or seed coat part

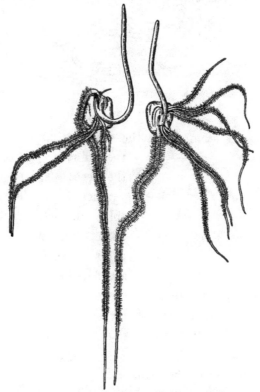

FIG. 21. Still later stage of Fig. 18. Note root hairs in all.

way, but not enough for the rest of the plant to escape. The little plant develops a curious contrivance to assist it in getting out. There is formed on one side of the

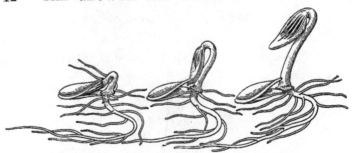

FIG. 22.   Pumpkin seedlings casting the seed coats (note the "peg").

stem a "peg" or "heel." This is formed on the underside of the stem, when the seed is lying on its side, at

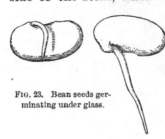

FIG. 23.   Bean seeds germinating under glass.

the point in the opening of
the seed. This peg presses
against the end and helps to
split the seed coat further
open. The stem now elon-
gates above this peg, presses
against the other half of the

seed coat, and pries the two
halves far apart so that the
plant readily slips out, as shown
in Fig. 22.

Germination of the bean. After
the root comes out of the bean

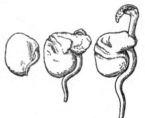

FIG. 24.   Peas germinating
under glass.

FIG. 25.   Sunflower
seed germinating.

on the concave
side, the two halves
of the bean swell so that the outer coat
is cracked and begins to slip off. We can

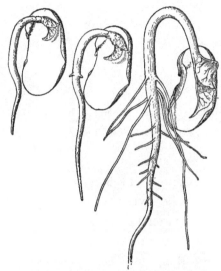

then see that the
stem is a continua-
tion above from the
root, joined to one
end of the two thick
parts or cotyledons.
This part of the stem
now grows rapidly,

FIG. 26. Beans with one cotyledon removed to see
how the cotyledons are raised up from the ground.

arches up in a loop,
and lifts the bean
upward.

The pea. The
pea germinates in
a different way.
After the root be-
gins to grow the
pea swells, so that
the thin coat is cracked. The stem, just as in
the bean, is joined at one side to the two thick
cotyledons of the pea. But this part of the

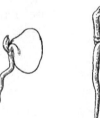

FIG. 27. Peas with one cotyledon removed
to see how the cotyledons are left in the
ground.

stem of the pea does not grow longer, so the pea is left
in position in the ground.   The stem grows on from
between the two

thick cotyledons,
arches up in a loop,
pulls out the young
and tender leaves

FIG. 28.   White oak acorns germinating.

from the ground, and then straightens up.

**To compare the germination of the bean with
that of the pea.**   This can be done very easily by first
soaking beans and peas for twenty-four hours in water.

With the finger or with the knife split
the bean along the line of the convex
side and pull the halves apart.   The

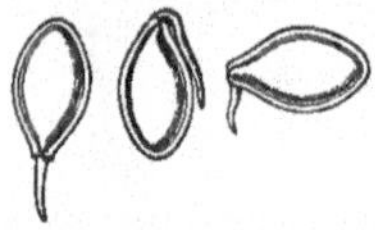

FIG. 29. Pumpkin seeds
germinating under
glass, turned in dif-
ferent positions.

young embryo plant lies attached to
one of these halves, having broken
away from the other.   Split several
beans in the same way and place the half which has
the embryo bean plant under glass, in position as shown
in Fig. 26.

Take one of the peas and, by a slight
rubbing pressure between the fingers,
remove the thin outer coat.   The split
between the halves is now seen.   Carefully break away one of these halves

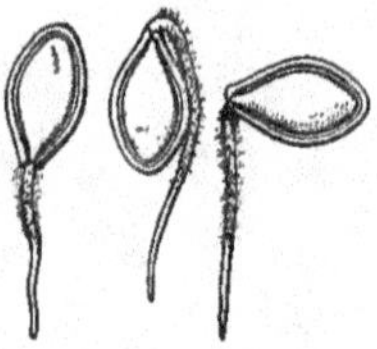

FIG. 30. Same as Fig. 29,
but later stage.

and split several more peas in the same way; those
pieces which have the embryo attached should be planted

under glass near the beans, in position as shown in Fig. 27. From day to day observe the growth in each case. That part of the bean stem below the cotyledon can be seen to elongate, while in the pea it is the stem above the attachment of the coty-ledon which grows.

The oak seedling. The young oak plant comes out of the acorn in a curious way. It is easy to get the acorns to see how they behave. Visit a white oak tree in late October several weeks after the acorns have been falling from the tree. If the tree is situated by the roadside, or

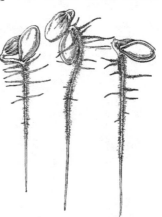

FIG. 31. Later stage of Fig. 29.

in a field where there is some loose earth which is damp and shaded, many of the acorns will be partially buried in the soil. Or you may collect the acorns and half bury them in a cool, damp soil, which should be watered from time to time.

The root is the first to appear, and it comes out of the small end of the acorn, splitting the short point on the end of the seed in a star-shaped fashion. The root immediately turns downward, so that if the acorn is not buried the root will soon reach the soil. This can be seen in Fig. 28.

How the oak seedling escapes from the acorn.   If you look for sprouted acorns, you will find them in different stages of growth.   Some with the root just emerging will be found, and others with the "tail" an inch or more long. In these larger ones we can see that the part next the acorn is split into two parts. As it curves, this split often widens, so that we can see in between. In such cases a tiny bud may be seen lying close in the fork of the two parts. This bud is the growing end of the stem, and we now see that the tiny plant backed out of the acorn.

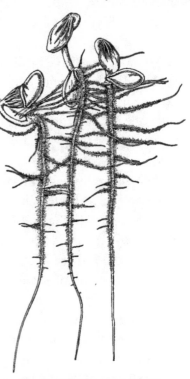

FIG. 32.   Still later stage of Fig. 29.

The root hairs.   In this study of the seedlings grown under a glass, or in a box or vessel where there is no soil for the root to bury itself, you will see that the root soon becomes covered, a little distance back of the tip, with a dense white woolly or fuzzy growth. You will see that these are like very tiny hairs, and that the root bristles all around with them. They are the *root hairs*. They help the root to do its work, as we shall see in a later study.

CHAPTER III

THE PARTS OF THE SEED

Are the parts of the seedling present in the seed?
Since the root comes from the seed so soon after planting, when the soil is moist and the weather warm, and the other parts quickly follow, one begins to suspect that these parts are already formed in the dry seed. We are curious to know if this is so. We are eager to examine the seeds and see. The dry seeds might be examined, but they are easier to open if they are first soaked in water from twelve to twenty-four hours. When they are ready, let us open them and read their story.

The parts of the bean seed. The bean seed can be split, as described on page 14, into halves by cutting through the thin coat along the ridge on the rounded or convex side. Spread the two parts out flat and study them. The two large white fleshy objects which are now exposed we recognize as the two cotyledons which were lifted from the soil by the loop. The thin coat which enclosed them is the *seed coat*.

FIG. 33. Bean showing scar.

Lying along the edge near the end of one of the cotyledons is a small object which looks like a tiny plant.

18

Is this the *embryo* of the bean plant? The pointed end is the root, and we see that it lies in such a position

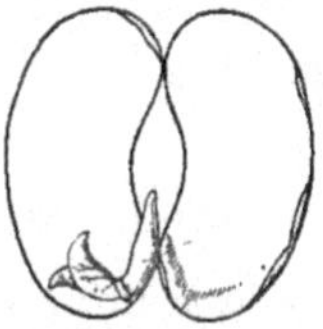

FIG. 34. Bean seed split open to show plantlet.

that when it begins to grow it will come through thé seed coat near the scar on the bean.

At the other end of the plantlet are two tiny leaves, pointed, and set something like the letter V. We know that they are leaves because there are veins on them like the veins on the leaf. Between these leaves and the pointed end or root lies the stem. It is short and stout, and there is *no distinct dividing line between it and the root. Root and stem in the embryo are called the* **cau-li-cle.** The upper end of the stem just below the tiny leaves is joined to the cotyledon, one cotyledon breaking away as the bean

FIG. 35. Cross section of bean showing situation of plantlet.

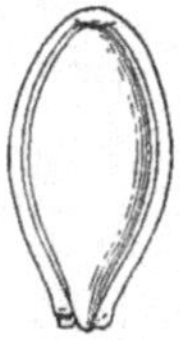

was split open. *The part of the stem below the cotyledons, that is, the part between them and the root, is called the* **hy'po-cot-yl.**

The parts of the pea seed. The position of the plantlet can be seen on one side of the rounded pea, below the scar, after the pea has been soaked in water. By a slight rubbing pressure between the thumb and finger the thin seed coat can be slipped off. The two thick cotyledons can now be separated. If this is done

FIG. 36.
Pumpkin seed.

carefully, the embryo plant remains attached to one of them.   Sketch this, as well as the embryo of the bean; compare them and indicate in the drawings the names of the parts.

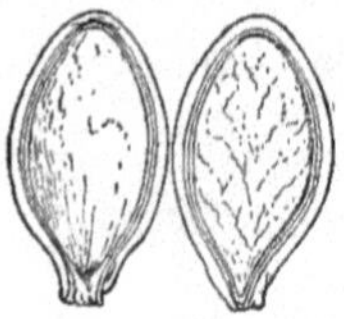

The parts of the pumpkin seed.   The scar on the pumpkin seed is found on

FIG. 37.   Pumpkin the smaller end.   The seed coat can be
seed split open; in
right-hand half split by cutting carefully part way
the papery covering around the edge of the flattened seed
shown which sur-
rounds the "meat." and then prying it open.   The "meat"

inside is covered with a very thin *papery layer*.   The pointed end of the meat is the *caulicle (root and stem)*. It lies, as we see, in the small pointed end of the seed coat.   The meat is in halves, as shown by a " split " which runs through to the point where they seem to be joined. *These halves of the meat are the* **cotyledons** *of the pumpkin*.   Pry them apart so that

FIG. 38.   " Meat,"
the embryo, with
one cotyledon
turned to one
side.

one is broken free.   At this junction of the cotyledons will be found a tiny bud on the end of the stem attached to one cotyledon after the other is broken off.   The

FIG. 39.   Long stem is very short in the pumpkin plantlet.
section through We have found in the pea and bean that it
a pumpkin
seed. lies between the cotyledon and the root.

So it does in the pumpkin.   Is it so in all seeds?

Cut a pumpkin seed through the cotyledons, but

lengthwise of the seed. Make a sketch of
one part showing the seed coat, the position
of the *papery lining*, the cotyledons as well as
the short root and stem. Cut a seed in two,
crosswise, and sketch, showing all the parts.

FIG. 40. Cross
section of
pumpkin seed.

The sunflower seed. The sunflower seed can be split
open to remove the seed coat in the same way as
the pumpkin seed. The meat occupies much the same
position, and is covered with a papery layer. While
the proportions are different, the general
shape of the plantlet reminds one of that
of the pumpkin or squash. The root and
stem are more prominent. There are two
flat cotyledons. As we spread them apart
we see that they are joined to the end of
the stem; we can also see between them
the tiny bud. If we cut the seed in two,

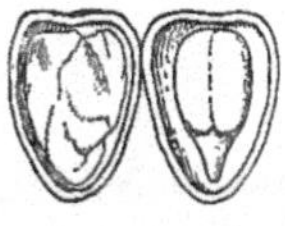

FIG. 41. Sunflower
seed split open
showing "meat,"
the embryo in right
and papery cover-
ing in left half of
seed coat.

as we did the pumpkin seed, we shall see that the
relation of the parts is much the same.

Structure of the corn seed. In the germination of
the corn we have seen that the root comes out at the
small end of the kernel in the groove on
one side, while the leaves first appear on
the same side at the other end of this
groove. If the tiny plant is present in
the seed, then it should be found in the
groove. Split the soft kernel lengthwise

FIG. 42. Embryo
of sunflower with
one cotyledon re-
moved.

through this groove. Just underneath the seed coat at
the small end will be seen the end of the root and stem

(caulicle).   Near the other end of the
groove there may be seen several converg-
ing lines running as shown in Fig. 44.

FIG. 43. Cross sec-
tion of sunflower
seed at left ; at
right, side view of
e m b r y o taken
from seed.

These lines represent several leaves cut
lengthwise while they are rolled round
each other.   The stem lies between the
leaves and root; it is now very short, and cannot be
distinguished from the root.   On the opposite side of
the stem from the groove is
a small curved object. *This
is the* **cotyledon** *cut through.*

There is only **one** *cotyledon*
in the corn seed, while in

FIG. 44. Section of corn seed ; at upper
right of each is the plantlet, next the
cotyledon, at left the endosperm.

the other seeds studied there are **two.**

The meat in the corn seed.   In the pea, bean, pumpkin, and sunflower seeds the cotyledons form nearly all

the meat inside the seed coats.   In fact,
the whole seed inside the seed coat in these
plants, except the papery lining, is the

FIG. 45. Long sec-
tion of b u c k-
w h e a t seed
showing one view
of embryo sur-
rounded by the
endosperm.

embryo, for the cotyledons, being the first
leaves, are part of the tiny embryo plant.
We have found something very different
in the corn.   *The embryo is only a small*
part of the inside of the seed.   After the seed has
germinated, the *food substance* is still there.   Did you

ever examine a kernel of corn after the seedling had been growing some time? There is scarcely anything left but the old and darkened seed coat. It is nearly hollow within. *The meat which formed most of the inside of the kernel has disappeared.* What has become of it? I think every one who has examined the corn in this way can

FIG. 46. Another section showing another view of embryo of buckwheat in seed.

tell. *It has gone to form* **food** *for the young corn plant. The substance which is used by the embryo for food is called* **endosperm**.

Is there endosperm in the seeds of the pumpkin, the bean, the pea, and the sunflower? That is perhaps a hard question for you to answer. It is a difficult matter to explain without taking a good deal

FIG. 47. Cross section of buckwheat seed showing coiled cotyledons.

of time. But I will ask a few more questions, and then perhaps you can guess. Where does the germinating pumpkin, sunflower, bean, or pea seedling find its food before it can get a sufficient amount from the soil? If from the cotyledons, or first leaves, where did they obtain the food to become so big in the seed? What about the papery lining in the squash and sunflower seed?

CHAPTER IV

GROWTH OF THE ROOT AND STEM

The part of the root which lengthens. One of the interesting things about the root is the way it grows in length. We know that as the root becomes longer the tip moves along. But does this take place by a constant lengthening of the extreme tip of the root? Or is the tip pushed along through the soil by the growth or stretching of some other part of the root? We can answer this if we examine the seedlings which are growing in germinators, as in the lamp chimney, where the roots are not covered with soil.

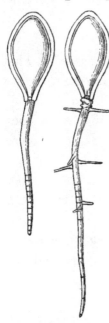

FIG. 48. Pumpkin seedlings, the root marked in left. Right one showing where growth took place in twenty-four hours.

To tell where the root elongates. Take a fine pen and some indelible or water-proof ink. Beginning at the tip of the root, mark off on one side very short spaces, as close together as possible, the first 1 mm. from the tip, and the others 1 mm.

24

apart, as shown in Fig. 48. Now place the seedling
back in the germinator in position, the root pointing
downward. In twenty-four hours see the result. The
spaces between the marks are no longer equal, showing
that stretching of the root takes place over a limited area.
Figs. 48 and 49 show the result with corn and pumpkin
seedlings. The root has not grown per-
ceptibly at the tip, for the space marked
off by the first line does not appear to be
any greater than it was twenty-four hours
ago. *Growth in length occurs in a region
a short distance back of the tip.* The
spaces between the marks back of the
tip, especially those between the third,
fourth, fifth, and sixth marks, are much
wider. This is the place, then, where
the root stretches or grows in length.

FIG. 49. Corn seed-
lings marked to
show where growth
takes place in the
roots.

The stretching is greatest in the middle of this region.

Direction of the roots of seedlings. The first root
from the seedling grows downward, as we have seen.
In the germinating seed, what advantage is there to
the plant in this downward direction of the first root?
The roots which grow out from this first or primary
root are called lateral roots. What direction do they
take? What advantage is there to the plant in the
direction which the lateral roots take? Look at the
root system, as a whole, of the seedling when well

developed.   What are the advantages to the plant of the distribution of the roots which you observe ?

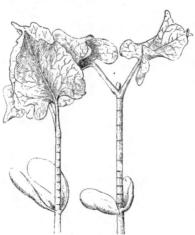

FIG. 50.   Stems of bean marked to show where growth takes place in stem.

Growth of the stem. In a similar way the region over which growth extends in the stem may be shown.   As soon as the seedlings come above the ground, or as soon as a new portion of the shoot begins to elongate above the leaves, mark off the stem with cross lines.   The lines on the stem may be placed farther apart than those on the root.   They may be put as indicated in Fig. 50. A rule may be used to locate the marks on the stem, and then, after several days, if the rule is placed by the side of the stem, the amount of growth will be determined.

CHAPTER V

DIRECTION OF GROWTH OF ROOT AND STEM

In our studies of the seedlings we cannot fail to observe that the *first root grows downward* and the *stem upward*. No matter which way the seed is turned, as soon as the root comes out it turns downward. It grows toward the earth, or if it is in the ground it grows toward the

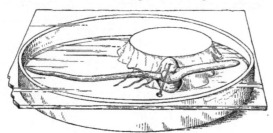

FIG. 51. Corn seedling pinned in a horizontal position.

center of the earth. So we say that the root grows toward the earth, while the stem grows away from the earth, or upward. It is interesting to notice how persistently the root and stem grow in these directions. To see how persistent they are in this, change the positions of the seedlings after they have begun to grow.

Downward growth of the root. Take any one of the seedlings germinated in moss or sawdust or behind

27

glass.   Place it in a horizontal position.   This may
be done behind a pane of glass in a box, or a pin may
be thrust through the kernel into a cork which is
then placed as in Fig. 51, with a little water in the bottom of the vessel
to keep the air moist.
In several hours, or on
the following day, ob-
serve the position of the

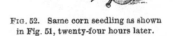

FIG. 52. Same corn seedling as shown
in Fig. 51, twenty-four hours later.

root.   The greater part of it remains in a horizontal
position, but the end of the root has turned straight
downward again.

**What part of the root bends when it turns from the
horizontal position?**   We should now determine what
part of the root it is which bends when it grows down-

ward in this fashion.   To
do this the root of another
seedling should be marked
and placed in a horizontal
position.   With a fine pen
and India ink, mark spaces
as close together as possible,
about 1 mm. apart, begin-
ning at the tip of the root.
Mark off ten such spaces, as

FIG. 53. Pumpkin seedling placed horizontally and marked to show where the
root bends when turning downward.

shown in Fig. 53, and leave the root in a horizontal
position for a day.   Now observe where the curve has

taken place. It has not taken place at the tip, for the mark made near the tip is still there. The curve has taken place back from the tip, in the region of mark 3, 4, or 5, probably, if the marks were close together at first. These marks on the bent region of the root are now far apart.

You remember that when the root was measured to see where growth in length took place, we found that the root grew in this same region, just back of the tip. This is an interesting observation, and I think you can understand why the root can bend easier in the region where it is stretching than in the region where elongation has ceased.

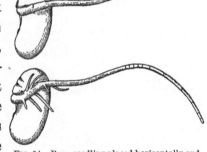

FIG. 54. Bean seedling placed horizontally and marked to show where the root bends.

The region of elongation is called the *motor zone*, because this is where the root moves.

What causes the root to turn downward? This is a question that is difficult, perhaps, to demonstrate to your satisfaction. It can be shown, however, that gravity influences the root to turn toward the earth. Gravity, you know, is the force which pulls an apple or a stone toward the earth when either is let fall. We must bear in mind, however, that gravity does not pull the root down in the same way in which it acts on the stone or apple. It only influences or stimulates, we say, the root to turn. (If desirable the teacher can

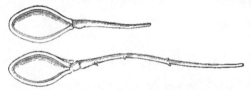

explain or demonstrate for the p u p i l s, that when the influ-ence of gravity is neutralized, the root does not

FIG. 55. Pumpkin seedling placed horizontally and root tip cut off to show that without the root tip the root will not bend.

turn downward but continues to grow in the direction in which it was placed. This may be demonstrated by the well-known experiment of fastening, in different positions, several seedlings on a perpendicular wheel or

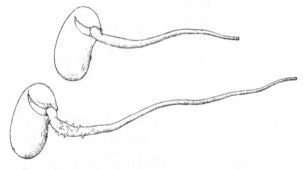

FIG. 56. Bean seedling treated as the pumpkin seedling in Fig. 55.

disk which revolves slowly. The position of the root with reference to the earth is constantly altered, and the influence of gravity is neutralized.)

If the tip is removed, will the root turn? Now place some more seedlings with the roots in a horizontal position, or, if you choose, this experiment can be carried on along with the others. With sharp scissors, or a very sharp knife, cut off the extreme tip of the root. In twenty-four hours afterwards observe the roots. *They have elongated,* **but they have not turned downward.** They have continued to grow in the horizontal position in which they were placed, although the motor zone was not cut away. Why is this? It must be that the tip of the root is the part which is sensitive to the influence or stimulus of gravity. For this reason the tip of the root is called the *perceptive zone.*

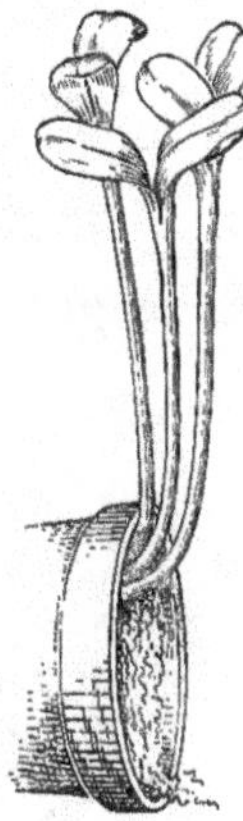

The upward growth of the stem. If the stem is well developed in any of the seedlings placed in a horizontal position, we see that the stem turns up while the root turns down. The corn seedling shows this well in Fig. 52. It is more convenient in studying stems to take seedlings grown in pots. Squash, pumpkins, corn, bean, sunflower, etc., are excellent for this study. Place the pot on its side. In twenty-four hours observe the plants. They have turned straight upward again, as shown in Figs. 57 and 58. In the case of the stems the part which turns is at a much greater distance

FIG. 57.
Sunflower seedlings turning upward.

from the end than in the root.   This is because the *region of elongation or motor zone in the stem is farther from the tip than in the root.*

How gravity influences the stem.   It may seem remarkable that gravity, which influences the root to grow downward, also influences the stem to grow upward.   It is nevertheless true.   The lateral roots and lateral stems are influenced differently.   What are the advantages to germinating seeds from this influence of gravity on root and stem?

Behavior of the roots toward moisture. Test this by planting seeds in a long box, keeping the soil in one end dry and in the other end moist.   The root grows toward moist places in the soil.   If the soil is too wet, the roots of many plants grow away from it.   Sometimes they grow out on the surface of the soil where they can get air, which they cannot get if the soil is too wet.

FIG. 58. Pumpkin seedlings turning upward.

CHAPTER VI

BUDS AND WINTER SHOOTS

Do buds have life? When the leaves have fallen from the trees and shrubs in the fall the forest looks bare and dead, except for the pines, spruces, cedars, and other evergreens. The bare tree or shrub in the

FIG. 59. Winter condition of trees and shrubs.

yard looks dead in winter. But examine it. The slender tips of the branches are fresh and green. If we cut or break a twig, it is not dry like a dead stick. It is moist. It seems just as much alive as in the summer, when the trees are covered with green leaves.

33

But look at the tip of the twigs, and on the sides, just above where the leaves were ! What do the buds mean ? Do they have life ?

How the buds look inside. On the shoot of the horse-chestnut see the overlapping " scales " on the bud. Take a pin and re-move them one after another. Observe how they are seated in the bud. On this side is one, and on the opposite side is another. How are the next two seated ? And the next ? They are not very easy to remove, and our hands are " stuck up " if we handle them. This sticky substance helps to hold the scales close together and keeps out water.

When the brown scales are re-

FIG. 60.
Shoot of horse-chestnut.

moved, see the thin chaff-like ones ! Then come scales covered with long woolly hairs. These scales are green in color, and in shape are like miniature leaves ! They are alive even in the fall or winter! How are they kept from being killed ? The long woolly hairs are folded round them like a scarf, and all are packed so tightly and snugly under the close-fitting brown scales

FIG. 61.
Shoot of lilac.

FIG. 62. Opening bud of hickory.

that they are well protected from loss of water during dry or cold weather, or after freezing. They lie " asleep," as it were, all winter. In spring we know they awake !

How the bud looks when split. With a sharp knife we will split the bud down through the end of the stem. We see how closely all the scales fit. Near the center they become smaller and smaller, until there is the soft end of the stem, which seems to be as much alive as in the summer, but it is resting now. The leaves in the bud are winter leaves. How convenient it is for the tree or shrub that in the fall it can put on this armor of brown scales and wax to protect the tender end of the stem !

FIG. 63. Long section of horsechestnut bud —scales and woolly scale leaves inside.

FIG. 64. Bud of European elm in section, showing overlapping of scales.

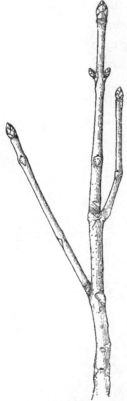

The lateral buds. There are several large buds on the side of the shoot, larger near the terminal bud. If we examine these, we find that they look the same inside as the terminal bud. The lateral buds are smaller, perhaps. Where are the buds seated on the shoot? The lateral buds are seated just above the scar left by the falling leaf. We say that they are in the axils of the leaves, for they began to form here in the summer, before the leaves fell. Are there buds in the axils of all the leaves of the shoot which you have?

Fig. 65. Shoot and buds of horse-chestnut.

Which buds will form branches next spring? What will the terminal bud do? Why is the terminal bud larger than the lateral buds?

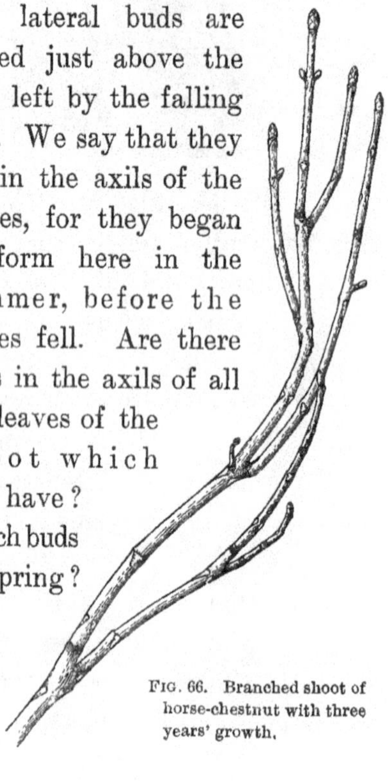

Fig. 66. Branched shoot of horse-chestnut with three years' growth.

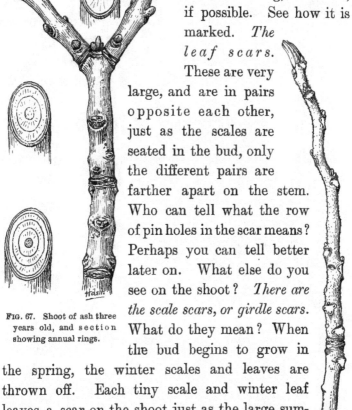

The winter shoot. You should have a shoot two or three feet long, branched, if possible. See how it is marked. *The leaf scars.* These are very large, and are in pairs opposite each other, just as the scales are seated in the bud, only the different pairs are farther apart on the stem. Who can tell what the row of pin holes in the scar means? Perhaps you can tell better later on. What else do you see on the shoot? *There are the scale scars, or girdle scars.* What do they mean? When the bud begins to grow in

FIG. 67. Shoot of ash three years old, and section showing annual rings.

the spring, the winter scales and leaves are thrown off. Each tiny scale and winter leaf leaves a scar on the shoot just as the large summer leaves do, only it is a tiny scar. But there are many scars close together all round the shoot,

FIG. 68. Shoot of butternut showing leaf scars and buds.

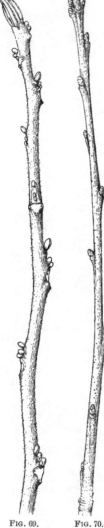

for, as we have seen, the winter scales and leaves are seated so in the bud. Each year, then, a girdle of scale scars is formed on the shoot. How old is the branch you have? Get a shoot which has several girdle scars on it. Cut it through, between the girdle

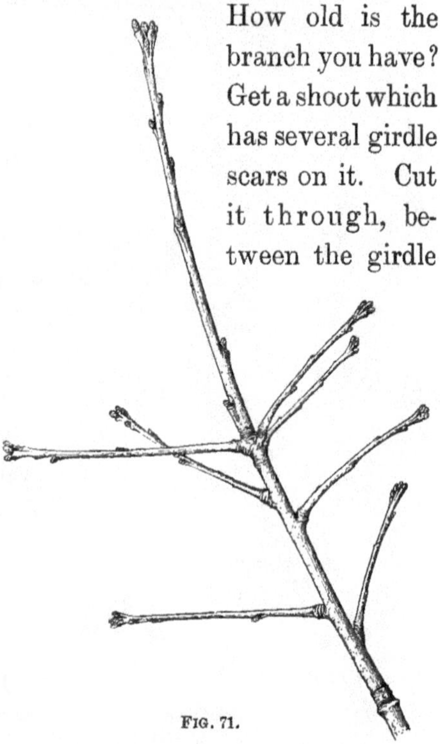

FIG. 71.

FIG. 69. Shoot of butternut showing leaf scars, axillary buds, and adventitious buds (buds coming from above the axils).

FIG. 70. Shoot and bud of white oak.

FIG. 71. Two-year old shoot of white oak showing where the greater number of branches arise.

FIG. 69.   FIG. 70.

scars. How many rings show in the cut surface of the wood ? What does this mean ?

Other buds and shoots. Gather other shoots and study the buds, the leaf scars, and their arrangement. Good ones to study are the ash, ailanthus, walnut or butternut, oak, elm, birch, dogwood, peach, apple, willow, poplar, etc.

Some buds may be made to open in the winter. Bring in shoots of dogwood, willow, poplar, ash, oak, etc. Rest the cut ends in water and see what will happen after several weeks or months.

CHAPTER VII

THE FULL-GROWN PLANT AND ITS PARTS

I. THE PLANT

The plant has different parts. The seedling has roots, stem, and leaves. The full-grown plant has the same parts. But the roots, of course, are larger, longer, and much more branched. There are many more leaves also, and the stem is often very much branched. Are there any other parts? There are the flowers, you say, and the fruit, and some plants have thorns, spines, hairs, and tendrils. Yes, but many plants have just the root, stem, leaves, flowers, and fruit. And how different they are in different plants! Did you ever notice that the form of the stem, and the shape and arrangement of the leaves and flowers mark the different kinds of plants so that you can tell them apart? The form of the entire plant we call its *appearance* or *habit*. *The seeds of each kind of plant make new plants of the same kind and shape.*

Tall, erect plants. The sunflower is tall and slender. At first there is a simple, straight, tall, shaft-like stem, and large, spreading leaves pointing in different directions.

40

At the top of the stem the first and largest flower head
is formed, and others come on later from short branches
in the axils of the upper
leaves. The full-grown
plant has a golden crown
of flower heads held up by
the tall stem shaft.

The mullein is also tall and
slender, with rough, woolly
leaves and a long spike of
yellow flowers. The plants
are tall and slender because
the main stem is so prominent and branches not at
all, or but little. In the
sunflower and mullein the
habit is *cylindrical*.

Tall larches, spruces, and
pines. These trees branch
very much. But observe how
small the branches are compared with the main shaft,
which extends straight
through to the top. The
habit is like that of a *cone*.

Fig. 72. Cylindrical stem of mullein.

The oaks and birches have a more or less oval habit.
The elms have a spreading habit, and so on. Is a pine,

or oak, or other tree different in form when it grows alone in a field from what it is when grown in a forest? Can you tell why?

Prostrate plants. The strawberry, trailing arbutus, and others are prostrate or creeping. You can find other plants which show all forms between the prostrate and the erect habit.

THE DURATION OF PLANTS

Annuals. Many of the flowers and weeds of the field and garden start from seeds in the springtime and ripen a new crop of seeds in late spring, in summer, or in autumn. Then the plant dies. It must be very clear to us that a plant which starts from the tiny embryo in the seed, forms the full-grown plant, flowers, ripens its seed in a single growing season, and then dies, has spent its life for the main purpose of forming the seed. The seed can dry without harming the young plantlet within.

Do you know that the seeds of many plants lie in the frozen ground all winter without killing the embryo? These plants live and grow, therefore, to form seed, so that their kind may be perpetuated from year to year. Plants which live for a single season we call *annuals*. Beans, peas, corn, buckwheat, wheat, morning-glory, ragweed, etc., are annuals.

Biennials. When you plant seeds of the turnip, radish, beet, carrot, cabbage, etc., a very short stem is formed the first season, with a large rosette of leaves close to the ground. No flowers or seeds are formed the first season. But if these plants are protected from the cold of the winter, the following season tall, branched stems are formed which bear flowers and seed. Then the plants die. The purpose of these plants, also, is to form seed and perpetuate their kind. It takes two seasons, however, to form the seed. Such a plant we call a *biennial*.

FIG. 73.   White oak, oval type.

The mullein is a biennial. The short stem and the roots live during the first winter.

Perennials. We know that trees and shrubs grow for a number of years. All but the evergreens shed their leaves in the autumn, or the leaves die. But new leaves come forth in the spring. Some of the herbs, like trillium, golden-rod, aster, Indian turnip, etc., produce flowers and seed each season. The part of the stem above ground dies down at the close of the season,

but the short stem under ground, or at the surface of
the ground, lives on from year to year. When the
seed germinates, the plant is so small at first, and even
for several seasons, that for the first few years no flowers and seed are formed. Those herbs which live for
several years, as well as the trees and the shrubs, we
call *perennial* plants. In these plants, also, so far as
we know, the main purpose of the plant, from the
plant's point of view, is to form seed and perpetuate its
kind. Plants like the cotton, castor-oil bean, etc., are
perennial in the tropics but become *annual in temperate
zones,* because the cold weather kills them ; they produce one crop of seed the first season.

Woody plants and herbaceous plants. The stems and
roots of trees and shrubs are mostly of a hard substance
which we call wood. They are often called woody
plants, while the herbs, whether annual, biennial, or
perennial, are herbaceous plants.

CHAPTER VIII

THE FULL-GROWN PLANT, ETC. (Continued)

II. THE STEM

What are some of the different kinds of stems that you can find in the field or wood, in the garden or greenhouse? There are many forms and shapes. *The stem of the sunflower is long and straight.* There are short branches at the top where the plant bears a cluster of large flower heads, the largest one on the end of the main stem. Did you ever see a sunflower plant with only one flower head? Can you tell why there is only one flower head sometimes? *The corn plant and the bamboo are good examples of tall and slender stems.* The corn tassel is a tuft of branches bearing the stamen flowers. The silken ear is another branch which bears the pistil flowers, and later the fruit. Are other branches of the Indian corn ever developed? *Wheat and oats, also, have tall and slender*

Fig. 74.
Sunflower,
cylindrical type.

45

stems. Perhaps all these plants have formed the habit of long stems because they often grow in large, crowded masses, and take this means of lifting themselves above other plants in search of light and air.

In the pines, spruces, and larches the main stem rises like a great shaft from the ground straight

through the branches to the top. The highest part is the end of this straight shaft. These trees have many branches reaching out in graceful curves, but the main stem remains distinct. *A stem which continues or runs through to the top is said to be* **excurrent.** Have you ever been on the top of a mountain surrounded by a forest of oaks, maples, beeches, pines, and spruces? You remem-

FIG. 75. Conical type of larch.

ber how the tall, slender pines or spruces towered above the oaks or beeches.

How is it with the oak stem? The branches are larger in proportion to the main stem, so that the main trunk is often lost or disappears. Compare the oak tree or pine tree which has grown in the open field with those grown in the forest. How should you account for the difference?

The trunk of the elm tree and its branches. Study carefully the way the branches of the elm are formed and you will see why the main stem is soon lost. *Such a stem is said to be* **deliquescent,** because it seems to be dissolved. Compare large elms grown in the forest

Fig. 76. Diffuse type of elm.

with those grown in the field. Why are they so different? Compare pines, spruces, and larches grown in the field with those grown in the woods. What are the points of difference and why? Why do the pines and spruces still have so different a habit from the oaks, elms, apple trees, and some others?

The strawberry, dewberry, and other prostrate stems creep or trail on the ground. *We call them* creeping *or* trailing *stems.* The strawberry vine takes root here

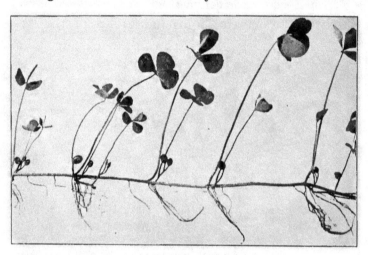

FIG. 77. Prostrate type of the water fern (*marsilia*).

and there and sends up a tuft of leaves and erect flower stems. The creeping water fern (*marsilia*) is a beautiful plant, the stem usually creeping on the bottom of shallow ponds or borders of streams, and the pretty leaves with four leaflets floating like bits of mosaic on the surface.

The pea, the Japanese ivy or Boston ivy, the morning-glory, and similar stems cling to other plants, or places of support. *They are* climbing stems. Then there are many stems which neither climb nor creep, nor do they stand erect, but are between erect and prostrate stems. Some *ascend;* that is, the end of the stem arises somewhat from the ground, although the rest of it may be prostrate. *These are* **ascending stems.** Others topple over so that the end is turned toward the ground. *They are downward bent* (**decumbent**).

Burrowing stems. Then there are stems which *burrow,* as it were. They creep along under the surface of the ground, the bud pushing or burrowing along as the stem grows. The mandrake, Solomon's seal, and the common bracken fern are well-known examples. The mandrake and Solomon's seal, and some others, as you know, form each year erect stems which

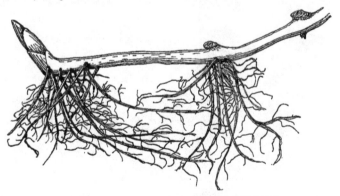

FIG. 78. Burrowing type, the mandrake, a "rhizome."

rise above the ground. *Stems which burrow along under the surface of the ground are called* **rootstocks,** *or* **rhizomes,** *which means* **root form.** They are known from roots because they have buds and scale leaves, though the rhizome of the bracken fern, the sensitive fern (see Fig. 93), and some others have large green leaves which rise above the ground. The trillium has a short, thick rhizome.

STEMS AS STOREHOUSES FOR FOOD

Bulbs are familiar to all of us. They are short stems covered with numerous overlapping thick scale leaves, as in the onion, the lily, or the tulip. Some bulbs, like the Easter lily, have a single stem. Some

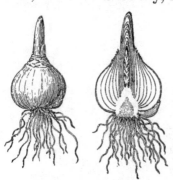

have several stems, like the Chinese lily, or the " multiplier onion." Quantities of food are stored up in the thick scale leaves, to be used by the plant as the flower and fruit stalk are being formed. In the Chinese lily there is so much food in these leaves

FIG. 79. Bulb of hyacinth.

that the bulb will grow if it is placed in a warm room with the lower surface resting on broken bits of crockery immersed in a vessel of water, so that the fibrous roots can furnish moisture. The lily will develop green leaves, flower stem, and flowers from the food in the scale leaves alone. These Chinese lily bulbs can be obtained from the florist and grown in the schoolroom or home.

Another kind of food reservoir for plants is the tuber. The most common and well-known tuber is the potato. It is a very much thickened stem. The " eyes " are buds on the stem. Do you know what develops from these " eyes " when the potato is planted in the warm ground? Place several tubers in cups of water so that one end will be out of the water, and set them in the

FIG. 80.   Tuber of Irish potato.

window of a warm room. Place some in a dark drawer where they will not freeze in winter ; leave them for about a year and see what will happen.

The potato is filled with starch grains. It is an underground stem. If you dig away the soil carefully from a " hill " of potatoes, you will see that there are underground stems more slender often than the erect ones, which have buds and scale leaves on them. On the end there is often a potato tuber. The starch is stored here for the good of the potato. New plants can be started from the tuber. They grow more rapidly and vigorously than from the seed of the potato. Man and other animals make use of the potato for food.

The short, flattened underground stem of the Jack-in-the-pulpit is called a **corm**. This lives from year to year. Every spring it sends up a leafy flower stem which dies down in the autumn. Young corms are formed as buds on the upper surface of the larger one,

probably in the axils of older leaves which have disappeared. These become free and form new plants. *Other corms are the* **crocus, gladiolus**, etc. To see how corms differ from bulbs, cut one open. It is a solid, fleshy stem, sometimes with loose, scale-like leaves on the outside.

Storehouses which are partly stem, partly root, are found in the pars-

FIG. 81. Corm of Jack-in-the-pulpit.

nip, beet, turnip, radish, etc. The upper part, where the crown of leaves arises, is the stem, and the lower part is root. *Such a tuber is sometimes called a* **crown tuber.**

Food is stored in rootstocks, or rhizomes, also, and in the stems of trees and shrubs. But the kinds enumerated above show some of the results which the plants have gained in forming special reservoirs for food. Most seeds, as we have seen from the few studied, are reservoirs of food so situated that the little plantlet can feed on it as soon as it begins to germinate.

CHAPTER IX

THE FULL-GROWN PLANT, ETC. (Continued)

III. THE ROOT

Taproots. In the seedlings studied we found that the first root grows downward, no matter in what position the seed is planted. This habit of downward growth in the first root is of the greatest importance to the plant to insure a hold in the soil where it must obtain a large part of its food and all its water. It also puts the root in a position to send out numerous lateral roots in search of food, and serves to bind the plant more firmly to the ground. In some plants the first root, or the one which grows directly downward, maintains this direction, and grows to a large size as compared with the lateral roots. *Such a root is called a* **taproot.** The taproot is a leader. You see it continues through the root system somewhat as the main stems of pines, spruces, etc., do through the

Fig. 82. Taproot of dandelion.

FIG. 83.   Fibrous roots of bean.

branches, only it goes downward. The dandelion is a good example. The turnip, carrot, and beet also have taproots.

The root system. The roots of a plant, with all their branches,

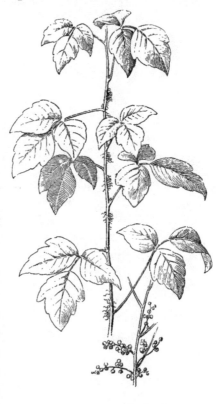

form the root system of that plant. Where the roots are many and all more or less slender, the system is *fibrous*, or the plant is said to have *fibrous roots*, as in the clover, the corn, wheat, grasses, etc. Where one or more of the roots are stout and fleshy, the system is *fleshy*, or the plant

FIG. 84.   Air roots of poison ivy.

FIG. 85.   Bracing roots of Indian corn.

is said to have *fleshy roots*. Examples are found in the sweet potato, the carrot, beet, turnip, etc. In the carrot, beet, and turnip the root is part stem (see page 52) and is called also a crown tuber. The fleshy roots of the sweet potato are sometimes called root tubers, because they are capable of sprouting and forming new potatoes. Examine roots of a number of plants to see if they are fibrous or fleshy.

Air roots. Most roots with which we are familiar are soil roots, since they grow

FIG. 86.   Bracing roots of screw pine.

in the soil. Some plants have also air roots (called *aërial roots*). Examine the air roots of the climbing poison ivy, but be careful not to touch the leaves unless you know that it will not poison you. One side of the stem is literally covered with these roots. They grow away from the light toward the tree on which the ivy twines, and fasten it quite firmly to the tree.

Air roots or braces are formed in the Indian corn, the screw pine, etc. Air roots grow from the branches of the banyan tree of India, and striking into the ground brace the wide branching system of the stems.

FIG. 87. Buttresses of silk-cotton tree, Nassau.

Buttresses are formed partly of root and partly of stem at the base of the tree trunks where root and stem join.

The work of roots. The roots do several kinds of work for the plant. They serve to anchor plants to the soil, or in the case of certain climbing plants to fasten them to some object of support. They aid also in supporting the plant and in holding the trunk or stem upright. Another important work is the taking up of water and of food solutions from the soil. In the absorption of water from the soil the root hairs of plants play a very active part. Pull up some of the seedlings growing in the soil and rinse the roots in water. If the smaller roots have not been broken off in pulling up the plant, particles of earth will be clinging to them which cannot be washed off. This is because the root hairs cling so firmly to the soil particles. This is seen in Fig. 91. When the soil is only moist the water in it forms a very thin film, as thin as the film of a soap bubble, which lies on the surface of the soil particles. It is necessary then for the root hairs to fix themselves very closely and tightly against the soil particles, so that they may come in close contact with this film of water.

FIG. 88. Root hairs of sunflower seedling.

FIG. 89. Root hairs of radish seedling.

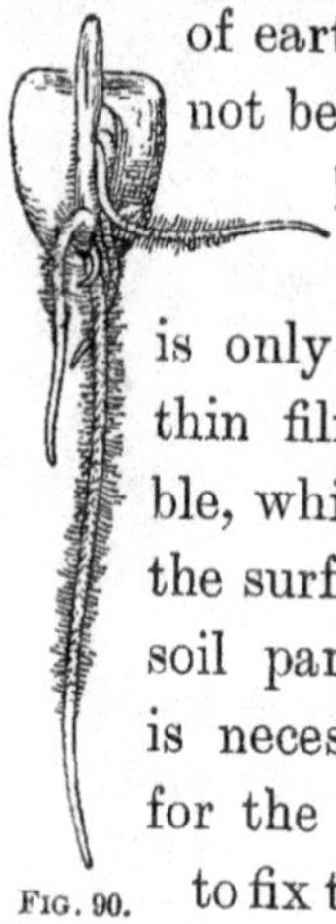

FIG. 90. Root hairs of corn seedling grown under glass.

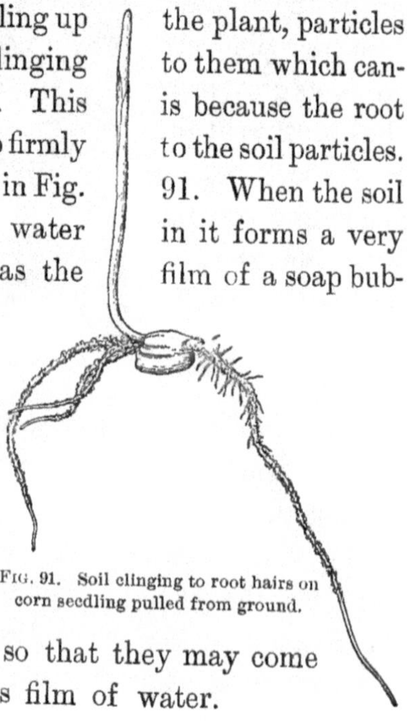

FIG. 91. Soil clinging to root hairs on corn seedling pulled from ground.

While plants need a great deal of water a great many kinds can thrive much better where the soil is moist, not wet. Most of the cultivated plants and many flowers and trees do better in well-drained land. Perhaps you have seen how small and yellow patches of corn or wheat look in the low and wet parts of a field. This is because there is too much water in soil and not enough air. On the other hand, there are a few trees and many other plants which thrive better in wet soil, or even in the water. It has been the habit of the parents and forefathers of such plants to live in these places, so they naturally follow in this habit.

How the roots and root hairs do the work of absorbing the water from the soil can be understood by the study of Chapters XI and XII.

CHAPTER X

IV. LEAVES

The color of leaves. In the spring and summer gather leaves of different plants in the garden, field, and woods. Examine those of many more. In the autumn or winter, plants in greenhouses or those grown in the room will furnish leaves for observation. What colors do the different leaves have? The oak, hickory, maple, elm, strawberry, dandelion, corn, bean, pea are all green in color.

Do you think that all leaves are green? Look further. Maybe you will see in some yard a copper beech, or birch, with leaves that are copper colored or brown, especially those that are on the ends of the new shoots. They are not so bright when they get older. They then show shades of brown and green. In the garden or in the greenhouse you may see leaves that are red, brown, or partly green and partly white. The coleus plant has variegated leaves, part of the leaf being green, and the middle part white (see Fig. 148). Many of you know the ribbon grass, striped white and green. **Why**

are leaves differing in color from the common green leaf usually found in the flower garden or greenhouse? Plants which grow in the fields and woods occasionally have variegated leaves, but they are rare.

If you should happen to find the Indian-pipe plant, or ghost plant, you would see that the leaves are white, or sometimes pink, but never green. They are very

FIG. 92. Purslane or "pusley" showing small thick leaves.

small. Has the dodder leaves? Yes, but they are yellowish white, not green. They, too, are very small. Do you know any other plants which always have white leaves? Are the leaves of such plants always small?

The green leaf, compared with white ones.[1] Compare the green leaves with the white ones. You see that nearly all the green leaves you have gathered, such as

[1] The leaves of plants grown in the dark are often white. This comparison should be made between leaves grown in the light.

those of the oak, elm, maple, apple, bean, pea, and corn, are broad and thin. The grass leaves are long and narrow, but they are thin. If you have gathered some pine leaves, or leaves of the spruce, balsam, fir, hemlock, or larch, you see how very different they are from the other leaves. Perhaps you have never heard of leaves on the pine, for they are often called pine needles, because of their needle-like shape. They are not so thin as most other leaves, and they are stiff. Did you ever see the purslane, or, as some people call it, "pusley"? Its leaves are not very large, and they are thick. So we find that while most green leaves are broad and thin, some are not. You see how quickly the thin leaves wilt and dry after they are picked. But the purslane leaves do not wilt so easily. On hot days, during a long "spell of dry weather," did you ever notice how many of the plants with green leaves wilt and suffer for want of water? At such times how is it with the purslane?

NOTE. — During late summer and autumn the leaves of many trees take on bright colors, such as red, yellow, etc., of varying shades. The pupils interested in gathering leaves will be attracted by this brilliant foliage. The beautiful coloring is the expression of certain changes going on inside the leaf during its decline at the close of the season. The causes of these colors form too difficult a subject for discussion here. But it should be understood that the "autumn colors" of leaves are not necessarily due to the action of frost, since many of the changes occur before the frosts come.

The Form of Leaves

Stalked leaves and sessile leaves. Most leaves are green. Most green leaves are broad and thin. You have seen this by looking at different kinds of leaves. Have you noticed the shapes of leaves? Yes, of course. You see the larger number of them have a little stalk (*petiole*) where they are joined to the stem which holds out the broad part (*blade*). In some of the water-lilies the stalk is long and large. In many ferns the stalk is also large and is sometimes taken for the stem (Fig. 93). But in many other leaves there is no stalk, and the blade is seated on the stem; such leaves are *sessile*. In some plants the stem appears to grow through the leaf, but in reality the leaf grows all round

FIG. 93. Sensitive fern showing large leaves and the rhizome or rootstock which runs underground.

the stem; sometimes there is one leaf only at one point on the stem, and in other cases two leaves which are opposite have their bases grown together round the stem.

Simple leaves and compound leaves. How many different pieces are there in the blade of a leaf? Look at the elm, the oak, the lilac, and the sunflower leaf. You see the blade is all in one piece, although the elm leaf is notched on the edge, and the scarlet oak leaf is deeply scalloped. Where the blade of the leaf is in one piece it is called a *simple leaf*.

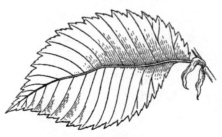

FIG. 94. Elm leaf (stipules where the leaf is joined to stem).

How many pieces are there in the blade of a bean leaf? a clover leaf? of the oxalis, pea, ash, hickory, and ailanthus leaves? If you do not find all these plants, you may find others which have leaves somewhat like them. Perhaps you thought each one of the pieces of the blade was the entire leaf. But see where the stalk of the leaf joins the stem. *The leaf stalk and all that it supports is one leaf.* We call such leaves as these *compound*. Do you know a compound fern leaf? The pieces of each compound leaf are called *leaflets*. Each leaflet is supported on the leaf stalk by a

FIG. 95. Compound leaf of ash.

stalklet. If you can find some of the different kinds of compound leaves, make drawings to show the shape, and

where the leaflets are attached to the leafstalk.   The
bean leaf, as well as that of the pea, ash, etc., is *once*

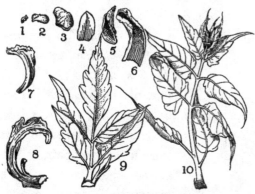

c o m p o u n d.
The leaves of
the sensitive
plant, of the
honey locust
a n d s o m e
o t h e r s, a r e
*t w i c e com-
pound*, and so
on.

FIG. 96. Scales, leaves and young summer leaves in opening
bud of ailanthus tree.

LEAVES WEARING A MASK

Masks on the pea leaf. Some of the leaves which
you have seen may have puzzled you because they have
parts which are not leaf-
like.   The pea, for
example, has curled,
thread-like outgrowths
on the end, which we
call *tendrils*.   These
tendrils cling to objects
and hold the pea vine
upright. Now see where
these tendrils are joined

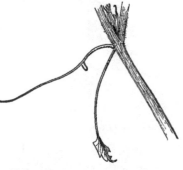

FIG. 97. Tendril of squash partly turned
to leaf.

to the leaf. They are in pairs, in the same positions as the leaflets. *Are they not leaflets which have changed in form to do a certain kind of work for the plant? Has the leaflet here given up its thin part and kept the midrib, or vein, to do this new work?* This part of the pea leaf is then *under a mask; it is disguised.*

Masked leaves of the squash or pumpkin. Examine the tendrils on a squash or pumpkin vine, or some one of their near relatives. Draw a cluster of tendrils and show how they are attached to the vine. Make a drawing of a leaf. Compare the two. Do the tendrils correspond to the large veins of the leaf? Did you ever find one of these which was part leaf and part tendril? Such leaves tell a very interesting story. Can you tell it?

FIG. 98. Awl-shaped leaves of Russian thistle.

Spine-like leaves. If there are barberry bushes growing in the yard, examine them. What position do the spines occupy? See the short, leafy branches which arise in the axil between the spines and stem. Is not the spine a mask under which some of the barberry leaves appear?

Not all spines, however, are masked leaves. Where do the spines or thorns occur on the hawthorn? Have you ever seen them on the Russian thistle, or on the amarantus, or pigweed, as it is sometimes called? What are the spines on a cactus? What are the spines on a thistle, like the Canada thistle or common thistle?

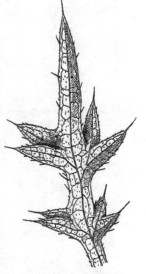

FIG. 99. Spines on edge of common thistle leaf.

The Position of Leaves

The plants in the field, forest, and garden, as well as those grown in the house, can tell some interesting stories about the positions of their leaves on the stem. The plants speak in a very quiet way. We cannot hear them, because they speak in a sign language. Now you know what this means, so you must look at the plants and see how the leaves are arranged. *The position of the leaves on the plant is the sign.* You are to act as the interpreter does, and put what the leaves tell into your own words.

One of the plainest signs which the green leaves make can be understood if you compare a geranium plant grown in the window with one grown out of doors, or

in a glass house where the light comes in from above as well as from one side. The leaf wants to face the light, to be in such a position on the plant that it can get light easily and directly on the upper surface.

In the corn plant, the sunflower, or the mullein, with erect and usually unbranched stems, the leaves stand out horizontally, so that they get light from the sky where it is strongest (see Fig. 72). You

FIG. 100.   Garden-balsam plant showing leaves near ends of branches.

see also that in most cases one leaf is not directly over another. They are set so that they do not shade one another. If two leaves are in the same perpendicular line, one is so much above the other on the stem that the slanting light can easily reach the lower one.

The garden-balsam plant, or the wild " touch-me-not," tells the same story and more. You see the stem is branched, and in an old plant all the leaves are near the ends of the branches, and on top. As the branch grew in length the leaves reaching out all around cut off much light from the center of the plant, and the leaves here, which were formed when the plant was younger, became so shaded that they died and fell away. Can you read this story in other plants ?

FIG. 101. " Feather down," elm.

The leaves of many trees tell a similar story. When the trees are in leaf observe how the leaves are arranged on the oaks, maples, elms, etc. You will see that the position of the leaves varies somewhat in different trees

of the same kind. The oak, or elm, or apple tree, which
has a great many branches, will have nearly all its
leaves on the outside. These allow so little light to
get to the inside of the tree that few leaves are formed
there. Have you seen trees of this kind on which there
were many leaves all through the tree and down its
large branches? What story is told by a tree which
has a great many leaves in its center? Did you ever
see a tall tree standing alone in a field or a yard, with
a great many leaves standing out from its trunk on
young branches? What story do they tell?

The story that leaves of forest trees tell. In the deep
forest all the leaves of the larger trees are at the top.
When these were very young trees, the leaves were near
the ground. The young trees had branches also near the
ground. Now the old forest trees show no branches
except near the top. They have long, straight, bare
trunks. The great mass of leaves in the top of the
forest tell us that they shaded the lower branches so
much that few or no leaves could grow on them, and
the branches died and dropped off. A little light comes
in here and there, so that the young trees in the forest
have some leaves on them. But do you see so many
leaves on young maples, pines, oaks, and other trees in
a deep forest, as you do on trees of the same size
growing in an open field? The forest also tells us that
there are some plants which like to grow in its shade ;

Fig. 102.   Mosaic of leaves of Fittonia, showing veins of the leaf.   The leaves present a beautiful broad side to the light.

for we find them doing well there, while they cannot grow well in the open field.

The duration of leaves. The leaves of most plants live but a single season. Most trees and shrubs shed their leaves in the autumn. Evergreen trees form a crop of leaves each season, but these leaves remain on the tree for more than a year, in some trees for several years, so that the trees are green during winter as well as summer.

The veins of leaves. If you examine carefully the leaves which you have gathered while learning the stories of their color and form, you will see that all of them have *veins*, as we call them. These show especially on the underside of the leaf as prominent raised lines where the leaf substance is thicker. There are large veins and small ones. The midrib of the leaf is the largest vein. The smaller veins branch out from the larger ones, or arise at the base of the leaf. If you look carefully at the leaves of some plants (*Fittonia*, for example, Fig. 102), you will see that the smallest veins form a fine network. The entire system of veins in a leaf forms the skeleton of the leaf. Where the veins form a network the leaf is said to be *net-veined*. Where the veins run in parallel lines through the leaf the leaf is *parallel-veined*.

You have observed the germination of the corn, and that it has *one cotyledon*. How do the veins in the

leaves of the corn run? In germinating beans, peas,
pumpkin, sunflower, oak, etc., you found *two cotyledons.*
How do the veins in the leaves of these plants run?

The work of leaves. Leaves do a great deal of work.
They do several kinds of work. They work together
to make plant food, and to do other work which we
shall learn later.

PART II

THE WORK OF PLANTS

CHAPTER XI

HOW THE LIVING PLANT USES WATER TO REMAIN FIRM

To restore firmness in wilted plants. We all know how soon flowers or plants wilt after being picked, unless they are kept where the air is moist. Many times we restore wilted flowers or plants to a fresh or firm condition by putting the cut stems or roots in water for a time. By a simple experiment one can show how to hasten the return of firmness or rigidity in the wilted plant.

Cut off several of the seedlings growing in the soil. Allow them to lie on the table for several minutes until they droop. Put the stem of one in a glass of water and place over this a fruit jar. Leave another stem in a glass of water uncovered. The covered one should revive sooner than the uncovered one.

How beet slices remain rigid. A beet freshly dug from the soil is quite firm. Cut out slices from the beet 4 to 5 cm.[1] long, 2 to 3 cm. broad, and about 4 to 5 mm. thick.   Hold them between the thumb and finger and try to bend them.   They yield but little to pressure.   They are firm or rigid.

Place some of the slices of beet in a five per cent salt solution,[2] and some in fresh water.   After a half hour or so, test the slices in the fresh water by trying to

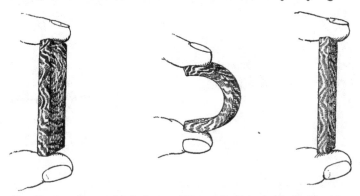

FIG. 103.   Beet slices ; at left fresh one, middle one after lying in salt solution, right-hand one taken from salt water and placed in fresh water.

bend them between the thumb and finger.   They remain rigid as before.   Now test those which have been lying in the salt solution.   They are limp and flabby and bend easily under pressure.

Now remove the slices from the salt solution and place them in fresh water.   After an hour or so test

[1] 2½ cm. = 1 inch.   25 mm. = 1 inch.
[2] Dissolve a rounded tablespoonful of table salt in a tumbler of water. The solution will be nearly a five per cent one.

them again. They have regained their rigidity. Instead of being limp and flabby they are firm and plump.

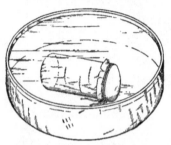

It appears from this that they
have regained their firmness
by taking in or absorbing
water. The slice of beet, like
all parts of plants, is made up
of a great many *cells*, as they
are called. These cells are
like tiny boxes packed close
together. Each one absorbs
water and becomes firm. Perhaps the following experiment will help us to understand how this takes place.

FIG. 104. Make-believe cell, with sugar
solution inside, lying in water.

A make-believe plant cell. Fill a small, wide-mouthed
vial with a sugar solution made by dis-
solving a heaping teaspoonful of sugar in
a half cup of water. Over the mouth tie
firmly a piece of a bladder membrane.
(The footnote, page 90, tells how to
get a bladder membrane.) Be sure that,
as the membrane is tied over the open
end of the vial, the sugar solution fills it.
Sink the vial in a vessel of fresh water
and allow it to remain twenty-four hours.
Then take it out and set it on the table.

FIG. 105.   Make-be-
lieve cell after
taking in water.

The membrane which was straight across at first is
now bulged out because of inside pressure.

Now sink the vial in a very strong sugar solution for several hours. There should be so much sugar in the water that all of it will not dissolve. The membrane has become straight across again because the inside pressure is removed. Now sink it in fresh water again. The inside pressure returns, and the membrane

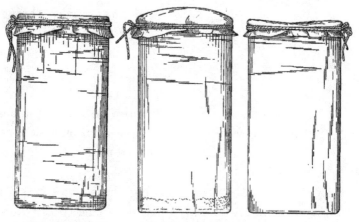

FIG. 106. Make-believe cell, at left before placing in water, middle one after lying in water has inside pressure, one at right after lying in very strong sugar solution has collapsed or become flabby.

bulges again. Thrust a sharp needle through the membrane when it is arched or bulged, and quickly pull it out again. The liquid spurts out because of the inside pressure.

What is it that causes the inside pressure? Why is the inside pressure removed when the vial is immersed in the stronger solution?

Movement of water through membranes. This experiment illustrates the well-known behavior of water and solutions of different kinds when separated by a membrane. Water moves quite readily through the membrane, but the substance in solution moves through with difficulty. Also the water will move more readily in the direction of the

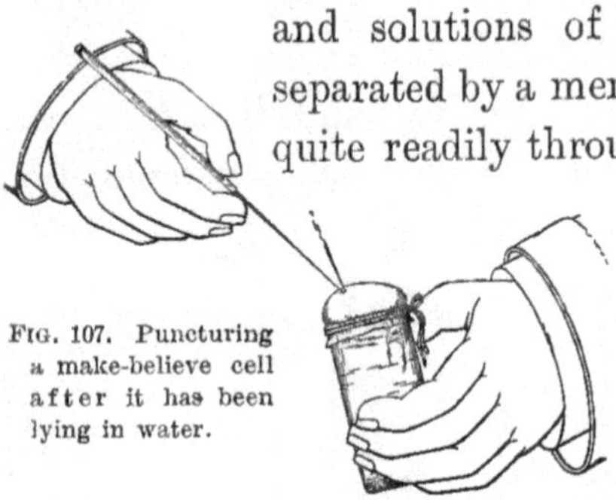

FIG. 107. Puncturing a make-believe cell after it has been lying in water.

stronger solution. The fresh water has no substance, or but little, in solution. The sugar solution is stronger than the water, so the water moves readily through the membrane into it.

Now when the vial containing the sugar solution is immersed in fresh water, some of the water flows through the membrane into the sugar solution, because this is stronger. This

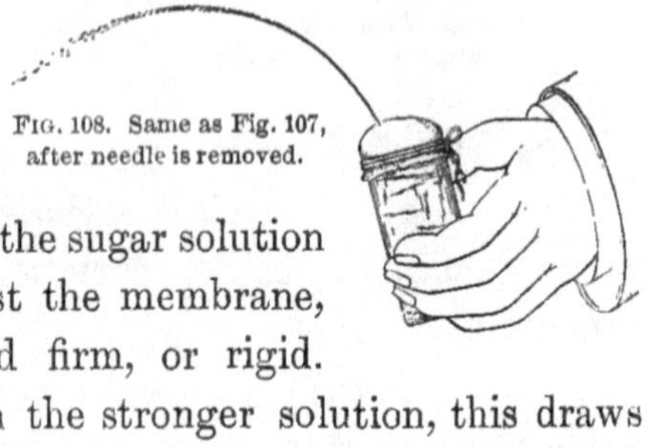

FIG. 108. Same as Fig. 107, after needle is removed.

increases the bulk of the sugar solution and it presses against the membrane, making it tight and firm, or rigid.

When it is placed in the stronger solution, this draws some of the water out, and the membrane, losing its firmness, becomes flat again.

How the beet slice works.   The beet slice is not like a bladder membrane, but some of the substances in the beet act like the sugar solution inside the vial.   In fact, there are certain sugars and salts in solution in the beet, and it is the "pull" which these

FIG. 109.   Picture of a real plant cell, at left it is in natural condition, middle one after lying in a salt solution, one at right after being taken from salt and placed in water.

exert on the water outside that makes the beet rigid. While these sugars and salts in the beet draw the water inside, what is there in the beet which acts like the bladder membrane through which the water is "pulled," and which holds it from flowing quickly out again? *In the beet slices there are thousands of tiny membranes of a slimy substance in the form of rounded sacs, each lining a tiny box.   Every one of these forms a plant cell, and*

FIG. 110.   Cells of beet slice, at left fresh, middle ones just placed in salt water, ones at right after lying in salt water a few moments.

acts like the bladder membrane in the make-believe cell. Inside these tiny membranes the sugars and salts of the beet are in solution.   When the cells are full and plump they press against each other and make the entire mass of the beet firm and plump. They are too tiny to be seen without the use of a microscope, but we can look at some pictures of them.

A dead beet slice cannot work. Place some of the fresh slices of beet in boiling water for a few moments, or in water near the boiling point. Then test them with pressure. They are flabby and bend easily. Place them in fresh cold water, and in about an hour test them again. They are still limp and do not again become firm. Why is this? *It is because the hot water killed all the tiny membranes in the beet, so that they cannot longer do the work. In the living plant, then, these tiny membranes are alive.* Yes, they are alive; and *really, they are the living substance of the plant.* Usually there are strings or strands of the same living substance extending across the sac like a rough network. The water in the plant, with the sugars, salts, etc., dissolved in it, is inside the sac.

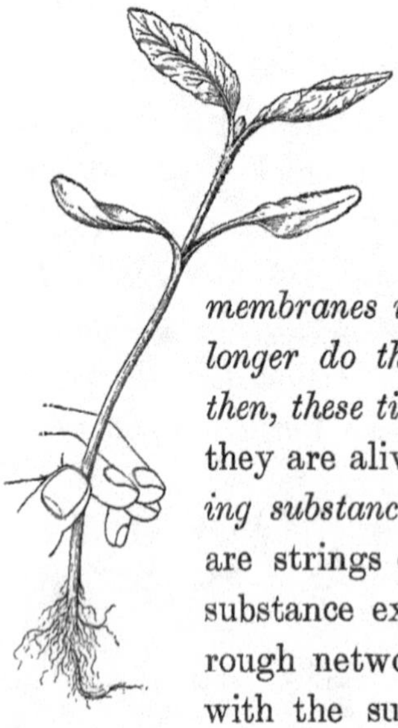

FIG. 111. Sunflower seedling fresh. It is firm.

Why the dead beet slice cannot work. When the living substance is killed the tiny membranes can no longer hold the sugars, salts, etc., inside them.

These escape and filter through into the water outside. In the case of the beet this is well shown by the behavior of the red coloring matter, which is also in the water, inside the tiny living membrane. When the living beet slice is placed in cold water the red coloring matter does not escape and color the water. Nor does the salt solution pull it out when we place the slice in salt water, although some of the water is pulled out. But when the beet slice is killed in hot water the red color escapes.

FIG. 112.   Same seedling as shown in Fig. 111 lying in salt water.

How other plant parts behave in salt solution and in water. Pull up a sunflower seedling or some other plant. It is firm and rigid as we hold it in the hand, and the leaves stand out well, as shown in Fig. 111. Immerse the leaves and most of the stem in a five per cent salt solution for fifteen minutes. Now hold it in the hand. It is limp and flabby,

FIG. 113.   Sunflower seedling taken from the salt water. It is limp.

as shown in Fig. 113. Immerse the seedling in fresh

water for half an hour and test it again. It has regained its former firmness, as shown in Fig. 114. Can you account for the behavior of the seedling under these conditions? How would it behave if we should immerse it in boiling water for a few moments? Why? Immerse it in alcohol for fifteen minutes. What effect has the alcohol had on it? Immerse a red beet slice in alcohol. Describe the results.

FIG. 114. Sunflower seedling taken from salt solution and placed in water. It becomes firm again.

Other plant parts may be treated in the same way, if it is desired to multiply these experiments.

The effect of too strong food solutions in the soil. Some of the plant foods are in the form of salts in the soil. If the salts are too abundant in the soil, the

FIG. 115. Sunflower seedlings after salt solution was poured in soil.

FIG. 116. Washing the salt out of the soil.

food solutions are so strong that the plant cannot take them up. In fact, too strong solutions will draw water from the plants so that they will become limp and will fall down, as shown in Fig. 115, where a ten per cent salt solution was poured into the soil. After these plants had collapsed, tap water was allowed to run through the soil overnight, as shown in Fig. 116. In the morning the plants had straightened up again, as shown in Fig. 117, because the excess of salt was washed out of the soil and the root hairs could then absorb water.

FIG. 117. After the surplus salt has been washed out of the soil the plants revive.

How some stems and petioles remain firm. Did you ever think how strong some stems and petioles must be to hold up so much weight as they often do? The pie plant or rhubarb leaf is very large, broad, and heavy. The

leafstalk, or *petiole*, as we call it, is quite soft, yet it stands up firm with the great weight of the leaf blade on the end. If you shave off one or two thin strips from the side, it weakens the leafstalk greatly. Why does the leafstalk become so weak when so little of the surface is removed?

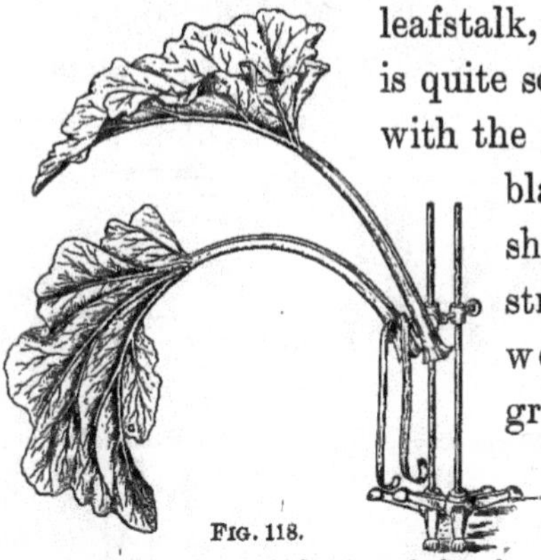

FIG. 118.

Leaf of pie plant (rhubarb) before and after shaving off two narrow strips from the leafstalk.

Cut a piece from a fresh leafstalk[1] six or eight
inches long. Cut the ends squarely. With a knife

remove a strip from one side, the entire
length of the piece. Try to put it in
place again. It is shorter than it was
before. Remove another strip and
another, until the entire outer surface
has been removed. Now try to put one
of the outside strips in place again. It
is now shorter than before as compared
with the center piece.

You see when the outside strip was
removed it shortened up. When all the
outside strips were removed the center
piece lengthened out. I think now you
can tell why it is that the leafstalk was so firm. Of
course it must have plenty of water in it to make the
cells firm. But the center piece alone, with plenty of

FIG. 119. Portion of
leafstalk of pie
plant with one strip
removed.

FIG. 120. Strips from outside of leafstalk of pie plant placed in water, at left they
coil up, at right in salt water they uncoil.

[1] If pie plant cannot be obtained, the plant known as Caladium
in greenhouses is excellent. In early summer the young soft shoots
of elder are good for the experiment.

water, is limp. You see when it is covered with the outside strips, as it is when undisturbed, the outside part is pulling to shorten the stalk and the center is pushing to lengthen it. *This lengthwise pull between the inside and outside parts makes the stalk firm.*

Why the dandelion stem curls. Did you ever break off a dandelion stem, press one end against your tongue, and make it coil up into beautiful curls as it splits? Do you know why it does so? Even when you split

FIG. 121. Strip from dandelion stem in water, at left it gradually coils up, in salt water at right it uncoils.

a stem with a knife or with your fingers it will curl a little. The inside part is trying to lengthen, and the outside part is trying to shorten. So when it is split it curls around toward the outside part.

Split a stem and place it in a vessel of fresh water. Watch it. It begins to curl more and more and more, until it makes a very close coil of several rings. *The life substance in the tiny cells takes in more water and swells so, that all together they push harder than they did before.* To prove this, put the strips from the dandelion stem in salt water. They begin to uncoil and finally become

nearly straight and quite limp. We know this is
because the salt " pulls " water out of the cells, just as

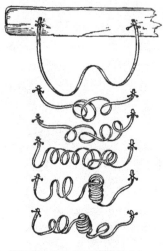

it does in the beet slice.
Now place the strips from
the salt water back into
fresh water. They become
firm and coil up again.

**How to imitate the coiling
of a tendril.** Cut out carefully a narrow strip from
a long dandelion stem.
Fasten to a piece of soft
wood, with the ends close
together, as shown in Fig.
122. Now place it in fresh
water and watch it coil.
Part of it coils one way and
part another way, just as a tendril does after the free
end has caught hold of some place for support.

FIG. 122.   Strip from dandelion stem
made to imitate a plant tendril.

CHAPTER XII

HOW THE ROOT LIFTS WATER IN THE PLANT

Root pressure in seedlings. To see this we may use the seedlings which are growing vigorously — sunflower, bean, pumpkin, buckwheat, and others. With a sharp knife cut off the stem near the upper end. In a few minutes a drop of water will be seen forming on the cut end of the stem. This increases in size until a large, round drop is formed. We know that water would not flow upward out of the stem unless there was some pressure from below. This pressure comes from the absorptive power of the roots. The roots, as we have found in our previous study, take up water from the soil through the root hairs so forcibly as to produce an inside pressure which makes the tissue firm. This water is passed inward in the root by a similar process until it reaches

FIG. 123. Drop of water pressed out of cut end of stem of sunflower seedling by work of roots.

minute vessels or tubes which are continuous with similar tubes in the stem. The continued pressure

which is formed in the roots lifts the water up and forces it out through the cut end of the stem. (The bleeding of cut stems in winter or early spring is due to changes in the expansion of the air, because of the great differences in temperature.)

Root Pressure in a Garden Balsam

The materials necessary for the study. Select a vigorously growing potted garden-balsam plant. If this is not at hand, use a coleus plant, geranium, or other plant. Select a piece of glass tubing several feet long and about the same diameter as that of the stem of the plant to be used. Next prepare a short piece of rubber tubing which will slip over the end of the glass tube. Then have ready some wrapping cord, a small quantity of water, a tall stake, and a sharp knife.

FIG. 124. Cutting off stem of balsam plant.

To start the experiment to show root pressure. With the knife cut off the stem squarely near the ground, as shown in Fig. 124. Slip one end of the rubber tubing over the end of the stem and tie it tightly with the wrapping cord. Then pour in a small quantity of water to keep the end of the stem moist at the start. Insert one end of the glass tubing in the other end of

FIG. 125. The materials for setting up the apparatus to show root pressure.

the rubber tube, tie it tightly, and then bind the glass tubing to the stake to hold it upright. The experiment must be made in a room in which the temperature is suitable for growth.

The result of the experiment. In a few hours the water will be seen rising in the glass tube. This will continue for a day or two, and perhaps for a longer time. The soil in the pot should be watered just as if the entire plant were growing. Observations on the

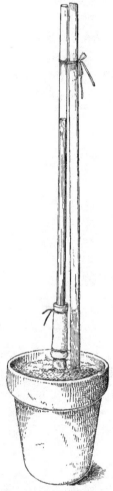

height of the water in the tube should be made several times a day for several days. It will be found that the column rises and falls, showing that there is some fluctuation in the pressure from the roots.

Thus we see that the roots by their absorptive power are capable, not only of taking in water from the soil with considerable force, but also of lifting it up to a considerable height in the stem. Root pressure, however, cannot lift the water to the tops of tall trees. It has been found that the root pressure of the birch can lift water 84.7 feet high, the grapevine 36.5 feet, and the nettle 15 feet.

A simple experiment to illustrate how root pressure works. Here is an experiment, easy to perform, which illustrates very well the way the root works in lifting water. Take a thistle tube (Fig. 127) and fill with a strong sugar solution. Tie tightly over the large open end a piece of a bladder [1]

FIG. 126. The experiment in operation showing water rising in the glass tube.

[1] Get one sheep's bladder, or several, at the butcher's and remove the surplus meat. Inflate,

membrane, after soaking it to make it pliant. Pour out from the small end enough of the solution so that it will stand but a short distance above the bulb in the narrow part of the tube. Invert this in a bottle partly filled with water, pass a perforated cork down the tube and into the mouth of the bottle to hold the tube in position, and bring the tube so that the sugar solution in the tube is at the same level as the water in the bottle. Allow this to rest for several hours.

If the experiment has been set up properly, the sugar solution now stands higher in the tube than the level of the water. Because the water in the tube has sugar dissolved in it, it is a stronger solution; that is, of a stronger concentration than the water in the bottle. In such cases, where the two liquids are separated by a membrane, more water always goes through into

FIG. 127. A "thistle" tube.

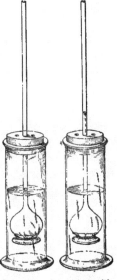

FIG. 128. Apparatus with thistle tube, bladder membrane, and sugar solution to imitate root pressure.

tie the open end, and place where it will dry. From these dried bladders a membrane can be cut whenever wanted. Soak in water before using.

the stronger solution. The bulk of the sugar solution is thus increased, and it is forced higher up in the tube.

The root acts much in the same way, except that each of the tiny root-hair cells and the tiny cells of the root act as the thistle tube and sugar solutions do, or as the make-believe cell did. The sap in the cells is a solution of certain sugars and salts. The life substance (protoplasm) in each cell lines the cell wall and acts

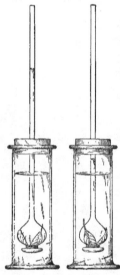

like the bladder membrane. The water in the soil is outside the roots, but comes in touch with the life membrane because it filters easily through the cell walls. So all the tiny cells work together, and the result of their combined work is like that of the thistle-tube experiment.

A potato tube may be used to represent the work of a single root hair, or of the root. Cut out a cylindrical piece from a potato tuber. Bore a hole nearly through it, forming a tube closed at one end. Place in the bottom of this tube a quantity of sugar and rest

FIG. 129. The same apparatus as shown in Fig. 128, but a leaf of a plant takes the place of the bladder membrane.

the tube in a shallow vessel of water. Observe how the sugar becomes wet from the water which is drawn through the potato tube. Does the water rise in this tube above the line of the water in the vessel outside? Why?

NOTE. — A living leaf of a plant may take the place of the bladder membrane. In the experiment illustrated in Fig. 129 the leaf of the jewel weed, or wild touch-me-not (*Impatiens*), was used instead of the bladder membrane. It is necessary to select a leaf which is free from any puncture, and it must be tied on carefully with a soft cord. In this experiment the sugar solution rose two or three inches in a day, and then rose no further. The thistle tube was then carefully lifted out, and the leaf was allowed to come in contact with boiling water to kill it. The tube was then replaced in the bottle of water. Strange as it may seem, the dead leaf worked much better as a membrane than the living leaf, and the sugar solution rose to near the top of the tube in two or three days.

CHAPTER XIII

HOW PLANTS GIVE OFF WATER

What becomes of the water taken up by the plant?
We have learned that the food which the plants take
from the soil is taken up along with the water in which
it is dissolved. We know that the solutions of plant
food must be weak, or the plant is not able to absorb
them. A large amount of water, then, is taken up by
the plant in order to obtain even a small amount of
food. We know also that water is taken up by the
roots of the plant independent of the food solutions
in it. It is of great interest, then, to know what
becomes of the large amount of water absorbed by the
plant. Some of the water is used as food by the
plant, but it would be impossible for a plant to use
for food all the water which it takes from the soil.

Loss of water by living leaves. Take a handful of
leaves, or several leafy shoots from fresh plants. Place
them on the table and cover them with a fruit jar, as
in Fig. 130. Place another jar by its side, but put no
leaves under it. Be sure that the leaves have no free
water on them and that the jars are dry. In the
course of fifteen or twenty minutes you can see a thin

film on the inner surface of the jar covering the leaves.
In fifteen or twenty minutes more it will be seen that
this is water, for it is accumulating in small drops

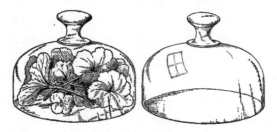

FIG. 130.   To show loss of water from leaves, the leaves just covered.

which become larger as the experiment continues.
The other jar is dry. The water, then, which first
formed the moisture film, and later the drops, on the
inner surface of the jar covering the leaves must come

FIG. 131.   After a few hours drops of water have accumulated on the
inside of the jar covering the leaves.

from the leaves. We see that it is not only on the
sides of the jar, but also on the top above the leaves.
So the water did not run off the leaves.

Further, we cannot see any sign of water until we see it accumulating on the jar, so that it must pass off from the leaves in a very light form, so light that it can float in the air like dust without being visible. When water is in this form in the air we call it *vapor*. *The water passes off from the leaves in the form of* **water vapor**.

Loss of water from living plants. In the above experiment the leaves were removed from the plant. It is not certain from this experiment whether the water passes off from the surfaces of the leaf or from the broken or cut ends of the petioles.

We are going to test the living plant in a similar way. To do this, place a potted plant under a tall bell jar, or invert a fruit jar over the plant, after having covered the pot and soil with a flexible oilcloth or sheet rubber, or several layers of oiled paper. Tie the paper close around the stem of the plant to prevent the evaporation of water from the soil or pot. During several hours the moisture film can be seen forming on the inside of the glass vessel. Gradually it accumulates

Fig. 132. Water is given off by the leaves when attached to the living plant.

until numerous drops are formed, some of which in time may trickle down the side of the jar. The

accumulation of the moisture may often be hastened
or increased at certain places on the jar by holding
a piece of ice near the jar outside. The cold glass
condenses the water vapor into water again, in the
same way that the cold air above condenses the water
vapor as it arises from the earth, first forming clouds
and later raindrops. *The living plant, then, loses water
through its surface in the form of* water vapor.

A delicate test for the escape of water vapor from
plants. A very pretty and delicate test for the escape
of water vapor from living plants can be made in this
way. Make a solution of a substance known as cobalt
chloride in water.
Saturate several
pieces of filter paper
with it. Allow them
to dry, and then dry
them still more thor-
oughly by holding
them near a lamp or
gas jet, or in a warm
oven. You will ob-
serve that the water
solution of cobalt
chloride is red. *The*

Fig. 133. A good way to show that the water passes
off from the leaves in the form of water vapor.

*wet or moist paper is also red, but when it is
thoroughly dry it is blue. It is so sensitive to moisture*

that the moisture of the air is often sufficient to redden the paper.

Take two bell jars, as shown in Fig. 133. In one jar place a potted plant, the pot and earth being covered as described on page 96. Or cover the plant with a fruit jar. Pin to a stake in the pot a piece of the dried cobalt paper, and at the same time pin to a stake, in another jar covering no plant, another piece of cobalt paper. They should be dried and entirely blue when they are put into the jars, and both should be put under the jars at the same time. In a few moments the paper in the jar with the plant will begin to redden. In a short time, ten or fifteen minutes, probably, it will be entirely red, while the paper under the other jar will remain blue, or be only slightly reddened. *The water vapor passing off from the living plant comes in contact with the sensitive cobalt chloride in the paper and reddens it before there is sufficient vapor present to condense as a film of moisture on the surface of the jar.*

The loss of water from plants. This is similar to evaporation, except that from a given area of leaf surface less water evaporates than from an equal area of water surface. It further differs from evaporation in that the living plant is enabled to retard or hold back the loss of water. This may be shown in the following way. Pull up several seedlings of beans, sunflowers, etc., and take some leaves of geranium or other plants. Divide them into two lots, having in the lots an equal number of the various kinds. Immerse one lot in boiling water for a few moments to kill the plants. Immerse the other lot in cool water, in order to have the living plants also wet at the beginning of the experiment. Spread both lots out on a table to dry. In twenty-four hours examine them. Those which were killed have lost much more water than the living plants. Some of them may be dried so that they are crisp. The living plants are enabled to retard the loss of water, so that the process of evaporation is hindered, not only by the action of the life substance within the plant, but also by a regulating apparatus of the leaves. *The loss of water from plants under these conditions we call* **transpiration.**

Does transpiration take place equally on both surfaces of the leaf? This can be shown very prettily by using the cobalt chloride paper. Since this paper can be kept from year to year and used repeatedly, it is a very simple matter to make these experiments. Provide two pieces of glass (discarded

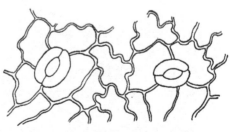

Fig. 134. The holes (stomates) in the leaf bordered by the guard cells.

glass negatives, cleaned, are excellent), two pieces of cobalt chloride paper, and some geranium leaves entirely free from surface water. Dry the paper until it is blue. Place one piece of the paper on a glass plate; place the geranium leaf with the underside on the paper.

FIG. 135. The stomate open.

On the upper side of the leaf now place the other cobalt paper, and next the second piece of glass. On the pile place a light weight to keep the parts well in contact. In fifteen or twenty minutes open and examine. *The paper next the underside of the geranium leaf is red where it lies under the leaf. The paper on the upper side is only slightly reddened.* **The greater loss of water, then, is through the underside of the geranium leaf.** This is true of a great many leaves, as tests which you can make will show. But it is not true of all.

Why do many leaves lose more water through the underside? You will not be able to see with your eyes the mechanism in the leaf by which it can, to some extent, control the escape of the water vapor. It is too tiny. It can only be seen by using a microscope to look through pieces of the skin, or *epidermis*, of the leaf which we can strip off. Perhaps it will be just as well for the present if you look at a picture of it made from the leaf. Fig. 134 shows little holes through the epidermis. These open into spaces between the cells inside the leaf. Two cells, each shaped like a crescent, if you take a surface view, fit in such a way around the opening that they stand guard over it. We call them *guard cells*.

During the day the guard cells are filled tightly with water and press back against the other cells and keep the little holes (*stomates*) open. At night they lose some of their water, so they are not so tight. They then collapse a little, so that their inner edges come together and close the opening. *The water vapor cannot escape so fast when the stomates are closed.*

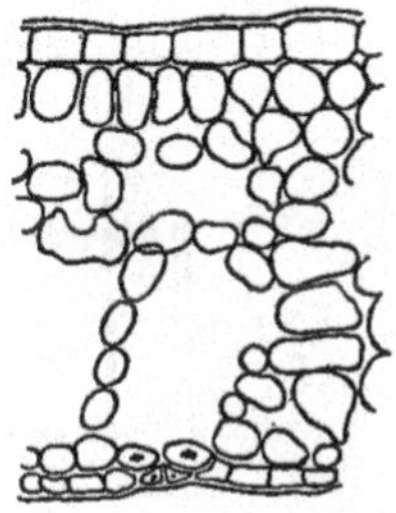

On very sunny days during dry weather, if the roots cannot give the plant enough water, the guard cells lose some of their water, so that they close up and prevent such a large escape of water as would take place should they remain open. Is this not a good arrangement which the leaf has to prevent the loss of too much water during dry weather? Sometimes, however, the ground gets so dry that the roots cannot get enough water for the plant. The plants then wilt, and sometimes die.

FIG. 136. The stomate closed; the air spaces in the leaf can also be seen.

Leaves help to lift water in the plant. As the water evaporates or transpires from the surface of the leaves more water is drawn up into the leaf to take its place.

This work is done by the tiny cells of the leaf. The leaf, then, can help lift water in the plant. This can be well shown by the experiment in Fig. 137. A leafy shoot of coleus, geranium, or other plant is cut, and connected by a short piece of rubber tubing

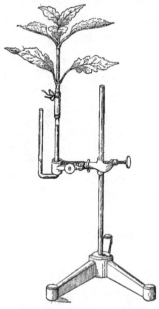

to one end of a bent, or U, tube which has been filled with water so that the end of the cut shoot is in contact with the water. The rubber tube must be tied tightly both to the shoot and to the glass tube, so that air cannot get in. As the water transpires from the leaf it is gradually drawn from the tube so that it lowers in the other arm of the tube. When the water is nearly all out of this arm, mercury may be poured in, and after a time the mercury will be lifted

FIG. 137. Showing that the leaf can raise water in the stem as it is given off at the surface.

higher in the arm of the tube which is connected with the plant than in the other. Mercury is a great deal heavier than water, so the leaves can do some pretty hard work in lifting.

Can the roots take the water into the plant faster than the leaves can give it off? Here is a pretty experiment to show the power of root absorption. Young wheat plants growing in a pot will show it clearly if the pot is covered with a fruit jar and the roots are kept warm. Fig. 138 shows how this can be done. If it is not summer time, when the soil in the pot would be quite warm enough, the pot may be set in a broad pan of wet moss or sawdust, and here covered with the fruit jar. A flame from a spirit lamp may be set so that it will warm the edge of the pan, but the soil in the pot must not be allowed to

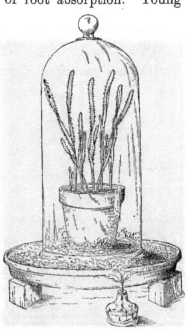

FIG. 138. The roots are lifting more water into the plant than can be given off in the form of water vapor, so it is pressed out in drops.

get hot. In a few hours or a day the leaves will appear beaded with the drops of water which are pressed out. There are little holes on the edge of the leaf through which the water escapes. These are *water stomates*.

This condition of things sometimes happens at night when the soil is warm and the air damp and cool, so that the green leaves cannot transpire rapidly. *We say, then, that* **root pressure exceeds transpiration.** *When a plant wilts on a hot, dry day, it is transpiring faster than the roots can lift up water, because there is so little water in the dry soil.* **Transpiration now exceeds root pressure.**

CHAPTER XIV

THE WATER PATH IN PLANTS

How to determine the water path. You will be interested to find the paths by which so much water flows through the plant. These may be shown in a very easy way. You may cut some garden-balsam plants, or the wild *Impatiens* or jewel weed, or similar plants. These are very good ones for the purpose. Cut also some shoots of begonia or other plant with white flowers. If there are corn plants or wheat plants half grown at hand, some of these should be used. Use also some good bleached celery leaves cut from a bunch.

Fig. 139. Shoots of garden balsam, begonia, and pea, in colored solution.

Set these shoots in a vessel containing red ink. Or if preferred a red dye can be made by dissolving one of the red " diamond dyes " in water. In a few hours, sometimes, the plants will show the red color in the leaves, or in the white petals. At least in a day they will begin to show the red color.

There are several distinct water paths in the shoot.
This shows us in a very clear way that the red dye is
taken up along with the water and stains
the plant. In the garden balsam or the
jewel weed we can sometimes see red
streaks in the shoot by looking at the
outside. These mark the paths through
which the water flows. They are better
seen if we cut one of these colored shoots
in two. In the cut shoot they will show
as small round red spots where the colored
water has passed. In splitting the stem
they would appear as long red streaks or

FIG. 140. Portion
of stem of garden
balsam. The col-
ored tracts show
through the
outside of the
stem.

bundles. *In these bundles there are tiny
tubes or vessels, through which the water
flows. Therefore we call the water paths
in plants* **vascular bundles.**

The arrangement of the vascular bundles.
In cutting across the shoot of the garden
balsam, or coleus, or begonia, you will see
that these bundles have a regular arrangement. They are in the form of a ring.
These plants are annuals, that is, they live
only one year. There is but one ring of
bundles in them. If you look at the
stump of an oak tree or at the end of a log, you
will see many rings. Each year the bundle grows in

FIG. 141. Cut end
of stem showing
where the water
paths are located.

an outward direction as the tree becomes larger.   The
vessels formed in the bundle in spring and early summer

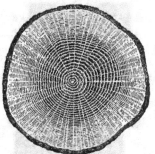

FIG. 142.   Cross section of oak, showing annual rings.

are larger than those formed
in late summer.   When cut
across in the tree these vessels
look like pores.   As all the
bundles in the tree lie close
side by side, the larger pores
formed in the spring alternate
each year with the smaller
ones and form a ring.   One
ring is usually made each
year as the oak tree grows, so that
the approximate age of the tree can
be told from the number of the rings.

The vascular bundles in a corn stem.
If a young cornstalk was in the red
ink, cut it across.   The red spots which .
mark the position of the bundles are
arranged irregularly.   If a fresh-
growing cornstalk is not at hand, take
an old dried one.   With a knife cut
around and just through the outer hard
layer.   Then gently break it, pulling
apart the two ends at the same time.

FIG. 143.   Vascular
bundles of corn stem
(where the water
paths are located).

As it breaks, the bundles pull out as stiff strings in the
pith, and in this way the irregular arrangement is easily

seen. A section of the stem of a palm shows that here, also, the vascular bundles are arranged irregularly.

Plants with netted-veined leaves usually have the vascular bundles arranged regularly in rings, while plants with parallel-veined leaves usually have the

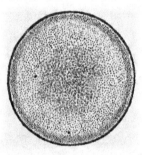

vascular bundles arranged irregularly. Compare the arrangement of the veins on the leaves of the garden balsam, coleus, begonia, bean, pea, sunflower, oak, etc., with the arrangement of the vascular bundles. The leaves are netted-veined, and the bundles are in regular rings. Compare the veins in a lily leaf or in a blade

FIG. 144. Cross section of palm stem. There are no annual rings.

of corn, wheat, oat, or grass with the arrangement of the bundles. The leaves are parallel-veined, and the bundles are arranged irregularly. You will remember that the bean, pea, oak, etc., have two cotyledons in the seedling, and that the corn has only one.

What kind of venation in the leaves, and what arrangement of the vascular bundles are usually found in plants with two cotyledons ? In plants with a single cotyledon ? What are these two large groups of plants called ?

CHAPTER XV

THE LIVING PLANT FORMS STARCH

All our starch is formed by plants. Starch is one of the essential foods of man and other animals. It is also employed in many useful processes in the manufacture or dressing of numerous useful articles. It occurs in many vegetables and other plant foods which we eat. Prepared starch, like cornstarch, used for puddings, is nearly or quite pure starch. All this starch is made by plants. The plants use it in a variety of ways for food, and much of it, after being formed, is stored in some part of the plant for future use, as in certain seeds, roots, or tubers. The potato tuber, for instance, is largely composed of starch.

Tincture of iodine colors starch blue. When starch is wet or moist with water it is colored blue by iodine. A tincture of iodine can be obtained from the drug store, or a few crystals of iodine may be dissolved in alcohol. In a test tube place a small quantity (as much as can be held on the point of a penknife) of cornstarch, which can be obtained at the grocery. Pour water into the test tube to a height of two inches. Hold the test tube over a flame for a few minutes to

warm the water so that the starch will be well wetted.
Now cool it by moving the end of the tube in cold water,
or by holding it in running cold water from a hydrant.
Add a few drops of the tincture of iodine.   The liquid

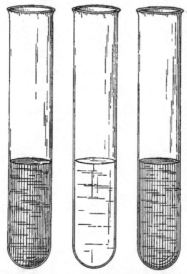

immediately appears blue
because the numerous
starch grains are colored
blue by it.   Now hold the
end of the tube over the
flame again for a few
minutes, but do not let it
get hot.   The blue color
disappears, because the
warm water extracts the
iodine from the starch.
Cool the tube again and
the blue color reappears.

To test the starch in a
potato tuber. Cut a potato
(Irish potato) in two, and
on the cut surface scrape

FIG. 145. Cornstarch dissolved in water,
and tincture of iodine added. At left the
solution is cold, middle one is heated
slightly, at right it is cooled.

some of the potato into a pulp with a knife. Apply
some of the tincture of iodine to the potato pulp. It
becomes blue. The potato, then, is largely made up of
starch. Place some of the pulp in water in a test tube,
and add a few drops of the tincture of iodine. Then
heat it gently to see if it behaves like the cornstarch.

Test for starch in Indian corn. Split a kernel of Indian corn and scrape out some of the endosperm or

meat. Place it in water and test with iodine. What is the result? Test grains of sweet corn in the same way. What is the result? The starch in the sweet corn was changed to sugar and stored in the seed in the form of sugar. The sugar beet is a reservoir for food. It is not stored as starch but as sugar.

FIG. 146. Variegated leaf of grass (white and green).

Starch formed in green leaves. Take a few green leaves which have been in the sunlight through the day. Immerse them over-night in a strong solution of chloral hydrate in the proportion of five ounces of chloral hydrate[1] to one-half a tumbler of water. This will remove the green color and the leaves become

FIG. 147. Variegated leaf of *abutilon*.

[1] Chloral hydrate can be obtained at the drug store, ten ounces for about one dollar. More accurately, use eight grams chloral hydrate to 5 c.c. of water.

pale. Rinse the leaves for a moment in fresh water.
Then place them in a tincture of iodine [1] made by dissolving iodine crystals in alcohol. In a few moments the
leaves become dark purple-brown in color, sometimes
nearly black, with a more or less blue or purplish tinge.
This is the color given to starch when it takes up iodine.
The experiment shows us that starch is present in the
green leaves which have been for some time in the light.

But if we should keep the plant in the dark for a
day or two, and then test some of the leaves we should
find no starch present.

FIG. 148. Variegated leaf of coleus plant, in fresh condition.

**Where starch is formed in the
variegated leaves of the coleus plant.**
The leaf of the coleus plant is
variegated, that is, it has different
colors. In this one which we are
to study, part of the leaf is green
and part is white, the green occupying the middle portion and the border, while the white forms a V
figure between. We wish to know
which part of the leaf forms starch.
We will immerse some of these variegated leaves in the
strong solution of chloral hydrate overnight. Now they

[1] The tincture of iodine can be purchased at the drug store. Or
one-quarter ounce of the crystals of iodine may be purchased and a few
placed in alcohol as needed.

are almost entirely white, the chlorophyll having been removed. We will rinse them a moment in water and then place them in the tincture of iodine. Those portions which were green are now quite dark, while the V-shaped figure, or that part which was white, remains white in the iodine or does not take the dark color. *The green part of the leaf, then, forms starch.* We have now learned that the leaf-green as well as sunlight is necessary to make starch. The leaf-green cannot make starch in the dark, nor can the light make starch in portions of a leaf which have no leaf-green.

FIG. 149. Similar leaf after green color is removed and treated with iodine to show location of starch.

Starch is formed in the green leaf during the day, but what becomes of it at night? In the afternoon let us cover a part of a leaf in such a way as to shut out the light from that spot. Take two corks, place one on either side of the leaf, covering a small circular portion, and thrust two pins through the edge of one cork to pin it fast to the other. From our former experiments we know that at this time of day all parts of the green leaf contain starch, so that the part covered by the corks, as well as the uncovered portion, now contains starch. On the following day at noon, or in the afternoon, we will take this same leaf, remove the corks, and immerse it overnight in the strong chloral-hydrate solution to remove the green color. Now we will rinse it and place it in the tincture of iodine. *The part of the leaf which was covered by the corks does not show the starch reaction, while the other parts of the leaf do.* So it must be that the starch disappeared from the leaf at night, that new starch was made in

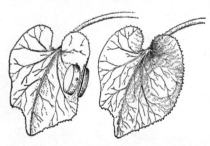

FIG. 150. Pumpkin leaves; at left portion of leaf covered to keep out sunlight; at right same leaf treated with iodine, no starch where leaf was covered.

the parts exposed to the light, and that no starch was formed in the part covered from the light.

When the starch disappears from the leaf where does it go? Is it found in other parts of the plant not exposed to the light? How does it get there, and where does it come from? For what purpose is the starch stored up in reservoirs?

CHAPTER XVI

THE WORK DONE BY PLANTS IN MAKING STARCH

Plants do work. It seems strange that plants work; yet it is quite true. Some plants do a great deal of work, and hard work too. Plants work when they make starch, though, as we have seen, they cannot do this work without the help of light. But light, without the leaf-green and the living plant, cannot make starch. We cannot see the work which the green plant does, but it is easy to see some of the signs which tell that the work is going on. We must learn to read the sign language.

How water plants tell of this work. Let us select some water weeds, or leafy plants which grow in ponds, lakes, or streams. A very good plant for this purpose is the *elodea*, but when this cannot be found others may be obtained which will serve quite as well. The plants may be brought to the room and placed in a bottle of water which is set in the window, so that they will get the sunlight, or the brightest light which may be had if the day is cloudy. In a very short time bubbles of gas collect on the leaves, small ones at first, but increasing in size until they are freed. Then they

rise to the surface of the water. Some of the plants
should be placed in an inverted position in the bottle so
that the cut end of the shoot will be below the surface.

From this cut end of the shoot bubbles
of the gas come out more rapidly than
from the leaves. Most of the gas, it
is true, came from the leaves, but
there are air spaces all through the
plant between the cells, so that the
gas which is formed in the leaves can
pass out not only at tiny openings in
the leaf, but also through the connect-
ing spaces in the stems.

**The more light there is the faster
the work goes on.** If the bottles containing these water plants are kept in
the window for several days, and there
is cloudy weather as well as sunshine,
you will notice that the bubbles of gas
come out more rapidly on a sunshiny

Fig. 151. The "tell-tale"
bubbles rising from a
water plant.

day than on a cloudy one. The more light there is,
then, the more work the plant can do. This can be
told in another way. Remove the bottle from the window and put it in a poorly lighted corner of the room.
The gas is given off more slowly. Cover the bottle
with dark cloth to shut out all light. In ten or fifteen
minutes uncover it. The escape of the gas has ceased.

Now place it in the brightly lighted window again. The bubbles soon start up afresh.

Do the "pond scums" do the same kind of work? Many of you have seen the green-looking "scum," as some people call it, which floats on the surface of ponds or on the water of ditches, and which is so abundant in the spring and autumn. This pond scum deserves a better name, for it is really made up of beautiful tiny plants, often consisting of silk-like threads, which we can see by lifting a bit of it from the water. To see that it does the same kind of work as the leafy water plant, place some in a bottle of water and set it in the window by the side of the other plants. The tell-tale bubbles show themselves here also. Now you have perhaps noticed that this pond scum, as it floats on the water, has a great many bubbles in it, caught in the tangle of threads. If you take up some of this tangle, rinse it in the water to remove all the bubbles, and then replace it in the water; it does not float well, but tends to sink to the bottom. But when the bubbles of gas begin to form again and are caught in the meshes of

FIG. 152. Bubbles rising from pond scum in sunlight.

the tangle, they are so much lighter than water that they buoy up the plant and lift it once more to the surface of the water. Here the plant can get more light, more air, and so do more work of various kinds.

The leaves of garden herbs and shrubs, trees, and other land plants do the same kind of work. But since they do not grow in water they do not show the signs of this work as water plants do. At least, we cannot see the signs of it because the gas is so much like the air in its nature. Perhaps you have put a lettuce leaf or a leaf of some other land plant under water, and have been told that the bubbles which rise from the leaf in the water are a sign that the leaf is doing work in starch-making. But this brings the land plant into an unfavorable environment, and it soon dies. Not all the bubbles given off are of the same kind of gas as that given off by the water plant, so that this must be regarded as a misleading experiment.[1]

[1] When the leaf of a land plant is placed in water there is always a thin layer of air over the surface of the leaf. If the water is exposed to the sunlight, there is a rise in the temperature which causes the air around the leaf to expand, and some of it rises in the form of bubbles. This may continue for a considerable time. Some of the air inside the leaf is also crowded out because of the change in temperature. This air that is rising from the leaf because of the change in temperature is not the same kind of gas that rises from the water plant or from the pond scum. We cannot distinguish between the two kinds of gas as they rise together from the land plant in the water. Therefore it is no sign that the plant is doing the work, but only an evidence that a change in temperature is going on which expands the air and causes some of it to be freed from the surface of the leaf. The same thing can be seen if we place a piece of broken crockery or a dry

What use the plant makes of starch. Since starch is
so necessary to plants, we ought to know some of the
uses which the plant makes of it. It helps to make
new life substance in the plant. This is necessary, not
only because more life substance is needed as the plant
becomes larger, but because, in one kind of work which
the plant does, some of the life substance is consumed.
We must understand that when the starch helps to form
new life substance it no longer exists as starch but is
assimilated along with other foods which the root takes
up. *The making of starch is not the making of the life*
substance. *It must be assimilated with the other food
substances taken up by the root from the soil, or by the
water plant from the water, before living material is
made.*

When we eat solid food substances they are acted
on by certain juices of the mouth, stomach, and other
organs. A part of the food is thus digested and dissolved. These food solutions are then absorbed through
the surface of the large intestine, where they enter the
blood. In the blood vessels they are finally carried to
all parts of the body, where they come in contact with
the living matter. The digested food is now assimilated

piece of wood in water, and then set the vessel in the light. To show
clearly that land plants do the same kind of work which the water plants
indicate by the bubble sign would be too difficult an experiment for
young persons.

and helps to make new living matter to replace that which has been used up in growth or work.

The case with the plants is somewhat similar, though their structure, of course, is very different. The starch made in the green leaf is the solid food, though it is not taken in by the plant in that form. It must be digested and changed to a form of sugar by the action of a juice (a ferment) in the life substance. Here it meets other food substances absorbed by the roots. Then by a process of assimilation similar to that which takes place in our own bodies, new living material is made.

So while plants and animals get their food by different methods, and in different forms, it is finally made into living material in the same way. The life substance of plants is the same as the life substance of animals.

CHAPTER XVII

THE KIND OF GAS WHICH PLANTS GIVE OFF WHILE MAKING STARCH

How to catch this gas in a tube. We are interested to learn more of this gas, and to know, if possible, what it is. We can catch some of it in a tube in the following way. We will take the *elodea* or some other suitable water plant. Place it in a tall, wide jar and invert a funnel over it so that the small end of the funnel will be under the surface of the water. Sink a test tube in the water, and then, without bringing the open end of the tube out of the water, invert it and lower it over the end of the funnel as shown in Fig. 153. Set the jar in the sunlight and leave it there for several days, arranging something to hold down the tube in case it becomes full of the buoyant gas.

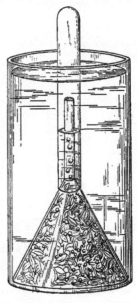

FIG. 153. Catching the bubbles of gas in a test tube.

121

The gas now, as it is given off from the water plant, rises through the funnel and into the test tube where it accumulates in the upper end and gradually displaces the water. In several days so much gas has accumulated that perhaps the tube is full of it and empty of water. We are now ready to test for the kind of gas.

How to test for the gas. We wish now to bring a glowing splinter into the end of the test tube before the gas escapes, and without wetting the splinter in

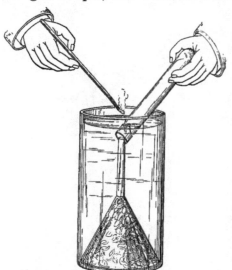

water. We light a long, soft pine splinter and hold it in one hand, while with the other we grasp the upper end of the test tube, which should be freed if it was tied down. Blow out the flame on the splinter, leaving the coal glowing. Quickly lift the tube from

FIG. 154. Ready to see what the gas is.

the water and thrust the glowing end of the splinter into the test tube. It flames again! The gas, then, is oxygen, for we know that the oxygen of the air is necessary in making a fire so that it will consume the wood, or coal, or other material.

The reason the glowing splinter does not flame in the air is because the proportion of oxygen is not great enough to ignite it. But there is so much oxygen caught in the test tube from the plant that the glowing coal readily flames again.

FIG. 155.   The splinter lights again in the presence of oxygen gas.

How is the gas formed? It is difficult to show here just how this gas is formed, for a considerable knowledge of chemistry is necessary to understand it thoroughly. But perhaps you have learned about some of the chemical compounds, as they are called, and how they sometimes change their combinations and associations. First let us boil some water. When it is cool, put a water plant in it and set it in the sunlight. No gas is given off. This is queer behavior, you may say. But it shows us that something was in the water which the boiling drove off, and which is necessary for the plant in order that the oxygen may be set free. This was air and carbonic acid.[1] If we introduce air and carbon dioxid into the water, oxygen will soon be given off again by the plant, since it can now absorb carbonic acid.

[1] The carbon dioxid is here in the form of carbonic acid, since it is in water.

How this takes place in land plants. In the case of land plants, the leaves of which are surrounded with air, not water, the plant absorbs carbon dioxid. You perhaps have been told that the air consists of about *twenty-one parts of oxygen gas, seventy-nine parts of nitrogen gas, and a very small fraction of carbon-dioxid gas.* The carbon-dioxid constituent is a chemical compound; that is, it is composed of two elements united. There is *one part of carbon* and there are *two parts of oxygen,* and it is written thus, CO_2. The carbons and oxygens hold on to each other very tightly, but so soon as they come in contact with water they quickly take up some of it and form carbonic acid. This explains how the carbon dioxid in the air for the land plants becomes carbonic acid in the water for water plants.

Water is a compound composed of *hydrogen, two parts,* and *oxygen, one part,* and its symbol is written thus, H_2O. As soon, however, as the carbon dioxid of the air is absorbed by the leaves of the land plants it comes into direct contact with the water in their cells, and forms immediately carbonic acid, just as it does when it dissolves in the water which surrounds water plants. The symbol of the carbonic acid then is CH_2O_3, since in the united compounds there is one part of carbon to every two parts of hydrogen and three parts of oxygen.

Now the carbon, hydrogen, and oxygen in the carbonic acid do not hold on to each other very tightly. When they get into the green of the leaf and the sunlight flashes in, it drives them apart very easily, and they hurry to form new associations or compounds which the sunlight cannot break. Perhaps it is because they hurry so, that the new associations they make are not permanent; at all events these are soon broken and others formed, until finally the elements unite in such a way as to form sugar in the leaf. The symbol for this sugar is $C_6H_{12}O_6$. To get this it was necessary for six parts of the carbonic acid to combine. This would take all of the carbon and all of the hydrogen, but there would be twelve parts of oxygen left over. This oxygen is then set free. From the great amount of carbonic acid which is broken up in the leaf under these conditions, a considerable amount of oxygen would be left over and set free from the plant. After the sugar is formed, one part of water (H_2O) goes out of it, leaving $C_6H_{10}O_5$, which is the symbol for starch.

CHAPTER XVIII

HOW PLANTS BREATHE

Do plants breathe? Yes. But if plants do not have lungs as we do, how can they breathe? There are many animals which do not have lungs, as the starfish, the oyster, the worm, etc., and yet they breathe. Breathing in animals we call *respiration. So in plants breathing is respiration.*

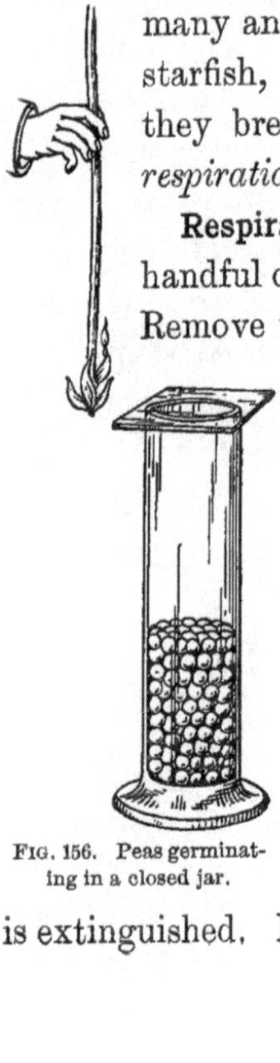

Respiration in germinating seeds. Soak a handful of peas for twenty-four hours in water. Remove them from the water and put them in a bottle or a fruit jar. Cork tightly or cover with a piece of glass, the underside of which is cemented to the mouth of the jar with vaseline to make it air-tight. Keep it in a moderately warm room for twenty-four hours. Keep an empty bottle covered in the same way. Light a taper or a splinter, and as the cover is removed from the jar thrust the lighted end into the jar. The flame is extinguished. Now light the taper again, uncover the

FIG. 156. Peas germinating in a closed jar.

empty bottle and thrust the lighted end of the taper
into it. The flame is not extinguished. A suffocating
gas, carbon dioxid, was in the first jar. This gas is
given off by the germinating peas. Being confined
in the jar, so much of it accumulated that it
smothered the flame.

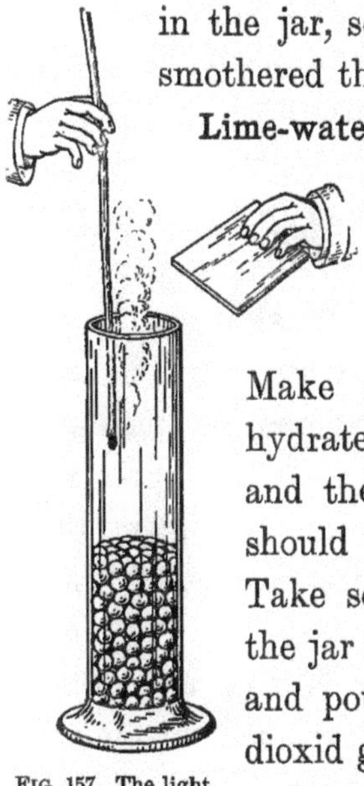

Lime-water or baryta-water is a test for
carbon-dioxid gas. Make some
lime-water by dissolving lime in
water and allowing it to settle.
Baryta-water is even better.
Make a saturated solution of barium
hydrate. Filter; or allow it to settle,
and then pour off the clear liquid. It
should be kept corked when not in use.
Take some in a shallow vessel. Open
the jar containing the germinating peas
and pour from it some of the carbon-
dioxid gas into the baryta-water. (The
carbon-dioxid gas is heavier than air and
therefore flows downward when the jar
is tipped.) Cover the jar again. Immediately on pouring the carbon dioxid into the baryta-
water, a white substance [1] is formed. Chemists tell us

FIG. 157. The light
is smothered in
the gas given off
by germinating
peas.

[1] Barium carbonate, if baryta-water is used, or calcium carbonate,
if lime-water is used. Lime-water is easier to obtain, but the results
are not so striking as with baryta-water. To make lime-water, take

that this white substance is formed by the union of carbon dioxid and baryta-water. Pour some of the baryta-water down the sides of the jar and on the peas. Notice the white substance which is formed.

Carbon dioxid from our breath. Take some of the fresh lime-water or baryta-water and breathe upon it. This same white precipitate is formed, because there is a quantity of the carbon dioxid exhaled from our lungs as we breathe. It is interesting to show this close agreement between plant life and animal life.

Plants take in oxygen gas while they breathe. Plants require oxygen in the process of respiration just as animals do. So far as the movement of the gases is concerned, respiration consists in the taking in of oxygen gas into the plant or animal body, and the giving off of carbon dioxid.

To show that oxygen from the air is used up while plants breathe. Soak some wheat for twenty-four hours in water. Remove it from the water and place it in the folds of damp cloth or paper in a moist vessel. Let it remain until it begins to germinate. Fill the bulb of a thistle tube with the germinating wheat. By the aid of a stand and clamp, support the tube upright,

a lump of lime twice the size of a hen's egg and put it in a quart of water. Allow it to settle and in a day or two pour off the clear liquid; cork in a bottle before using. The white substance formed when lime-water is used is due to the union of the lime-water and the carbon dioxid.

as shown in Fig. 158. Let the small end of the tube
rest in a strong solution of caustic potash (one stick
caustic potash in two-thirds tumbler of water) to which
red ink has been added to give a deep red color. Place
a small glass plate over the rim of the bulb and seal
it air-tight with an abundance
of vaseline. Two tubes can be
set up in one vessel, or a second
one can be set up in strong
baryta-water colored in the
same way.

The result. You will see that
the solution of caustic potash
rises slowly in the tube. The
baryta-water will also, if that
is used. The solution is colored
so that you can plainly see it
rise in the tube, even if you are
at a little distance from it. In
the experiment the solution in

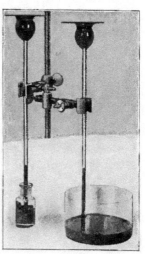

Fig. 158. Apparatus to show
" breathing " of germinating
wheat.

six hours had risen to the height shown in Fig. 158.
In twenty-four hours it had risen to the height shown
in Fig. 159.

Why the solution of caustic potash rises in the tube.
Since no air can get into the thistle tube from above
or below, it must be that some part of the air which
is inside the tube is used up while the wheat is

germinating.   From our study of germinating peas we
know that a suffocating gas, carbon dioxid, is given off
while they breathe.   The caustic potash solution or the
baryta-water, whichever is used, absorbs the carbon
dioxid.   The carbon dioxid is heavier than air, and so

settles down in the tube, where it can
be absorbed.

**Where does the carbon dioxid come
from?**   We know it comes from the
breathing, growing seedlings.   You
will remember that the symbol for
carbon dioxid is CO_2.   The carbon
comes from the plant, because there
is not enough in the air.   The nitrogen of the air could not join with the
carbon to make CO_2; so it must be
that some of the oxygen of the air
joins with the carbon of the plant.

Fig. 159. The same later.   Yes, it does; but the oxygen is first
absorbed by the plant.   When it gets into the living
plant substance, some of the carbon breaks away from
its association with the living substance and hurries to
join the oxygen, and together they escape into the air.

When plants breathe fast they are doing more work.
From what we have just learned we see that some of
the living plant substance is used up or consumed
while the plant breathes.   When a fire burns, oxygen

is taken from the air and joins with carbon in the
wood or in the coal, and carbon dioxid is set free.
This joining of oxygen and carbon is called *oxidation*.
In the living plant the joining of the oxygen from the
air with the carbon in the plant takes place slowly, so
that no flame or fire is made, but it is still oxidation.
Oxidation takes place slowly in animals in the same
way when they are breathing. But while the plant is
being partly oxidized or consumed as it breathes, this
very thing enables it to do more work, in growth
and in other ways. When you run or play hard, you
breathe faster. A part of your body must be oxidized
to get power or energy to play; or to work either, for
play is one kind of work.

The carbon dioxid which is given off is one form of
the waste from your body, or from the plant's body,
while work of this kind is going on. To take the place
of this waste you must eat, and you know how hungry
you are when you are growing and playing. You need
a great deal of food to make new living materials to
take the place of the waste, and to supply what is
needed for growth. So it is with plants; they need
food for growth, and to repair waste.

PART III

THE BEHAVIOR OF PLANTS

CHAPTER XIX

THE SENSITIVE PLANT

ONE of the most interesting manifestations of life in plants is the rapid movement of the leaves in the so-called sensitive plant (*Mimosa pudica*). The plant may be easily grown from the seed in pots, either in a

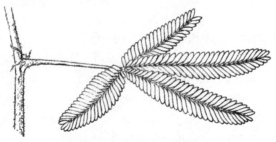

FIG. 160. Leaf of sensitive plant.

greenhouse or in the window of a room, if it is protected from the hot rays of the sun. The seed planted in late spring will bring forth good plants ready for use in late summer or during the autumn.

Appearance of the sensitive plant. The leaves of the sensitive plant are rather large. A leaf is composed of a large number of leaflets (*pinnæ*) arranged in pairs along four different axes, which are joined to a stalk (the *petiole* of the leaf) somewhat as the toes of a bird are joined at the foot. A single leaf is shown in Fig. 160 attached to the shoot. Imagine a branched shoot with a number of these leaves and you will know how the sensitive plant looks.

Movement of the leaves of the sensitive plant. When you wish to test the plant, it should be on a bright day, though the plant will work on a cloudy day also if it is not too dark. It must be left undisturbed and quiet for some time before using. We must be careful not to touch or jar it until we are ready.

FIG. 161. Movement of the leaflets after pinching one.

Now, with a pair of forceps, or with the fingers, pinch one of the terminal leaflets. Instantly the terminal pair clasp or fold together above the axis. Then the second pair do the same, and the third and fourth pairs follow quite regularly. This movement continues, successive pairs closing up until all on the axis are closed. Then the last pairs on the other three axes fold together, and successive pairs on these close up until all are closed. By this time, probably, the four axes which bear the leaflets are drawn closer together. The stalk of the leaf is also likely to turn downward, and the entire leaf presents the appearance shown in Fig. 162.

When we pinched the leaflet, there was given to the leaf what we call a *stimulus*. The stimulus travels all through the leaf, and in response to it the movement takes

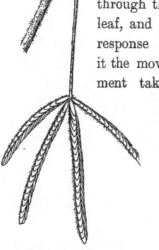

Fig. 162. Position of leaf after movement has ceased.

place. If we jar a sensitive plant suddenly, all the leaves close up and assume a drooping position, as shown in Fig. 163.

Fig. 163. The sensitive plant after jarring.

Behavior of the leaves at night or on dark days. On a dark day the leaves of the sensitive plant are folded together; or if we take the plant into a poorly lighted room, the leaves will close; then if we bring it out to the light they will open again. So at nightfall the leaves fold together, and the sunlight of the following day is necessary before they will open again. This teaches us one of the influences which light exerts on plants. This plant is very sensitive to contact with other objects or to shock; but we see that it is also sensitive to light, for the leaves will open in a short time when brought into the light. The *mimosa* is called the sensitive plant because it responds so quickly to contact stimulus or shock. In reality, however, all plants are more or less sensitive, some being more so than others. This we can readily see by observing the relation of other plants to the light.

CHAPTER XX

THE BEHAVIOR OF PLANTS TOWARD LIGHT

Compare plant stems grown in sunlight with those grown in darkness. When planting seeds of the sunflower, pumpkin, buckwheat, pea, wheat, or corn, etc., place some of the pots under tight boxes to exclude the light. The pots should be covered as soon as the seeds are planted so that no light will reach the young seedlings. They should remain covered for two or three weeks or more. They can be safely uncovered occasionally, for a few moments at a time, to supply the necessary water and to compare them with the seedlings started at the same time, in the light.

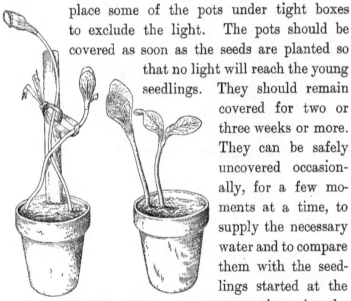

FIG. 164. Pumpkin seedlings: one at left grown in dark, one at right of same age grown in light.

Observe the plants about twice each week. Make measurements of the growth; sketch, and keep a

136

record of the observations. Do the stems grow more rapidly in the light or in the dark?   Com-
pare the leaves on the plants grown in
the dark with those grown in the
light.   Compare the leaves of the
wheat grown in the dark with those
grown in the light.   How does the
wheat differ from the pumpkin, sunflower, or similar plant in this respect?

Fig. 164, left-hand plant, shows a
pumpkin seedling grown in the dark.
The right-hand plant in the same
figure is another of the same age
grown in the light.   The stem grown in the dark is

FIG. 165. Buckwheat seedlings grown in light.

much longer than the one grown in
the light.   These plants are about one
week old.   Fig. 166 represents seedlings of buckwheat grown in the dark ;
they are longer than
those of the same
age grown in the
light.

Are the stems
grown in light
stouter and firmer?
In comparing the
seedlings grown in

FIG. 166. Buckwheat seedlings of same age,
grown in dark.

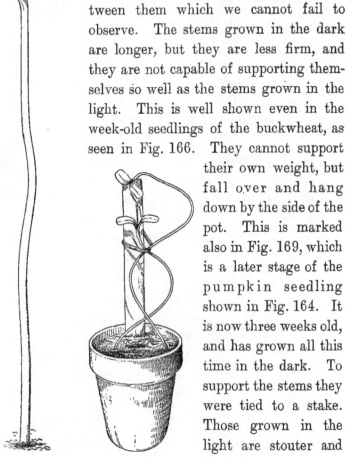

the dark with those grown in the light there is another striking difference between them which we cannot fail to observe. The stems grown in the dark are longer, but they are less firm, and they are not capable of supporting themselves so well as the stems grown in the light. This is well shown even in the week-old seedlings of the buckwheat, as seen in Fig. 166. They cannot support their own weight, but fall over and hang down by the side of the pot. This is marked also in Fig. 169, which is a later stage of the pumpkin seedling shown in Fig. 164. It is now three weeks old, and has grown all this time in the dark. To support the stems they were tied to a stake. Those grown in the light are stouter and firmer and are able to support themselves. If

FIG. 167. Sunflower seedling grown in dark. (Nat. size.)

FIG. 168. Sunflower seedlings grown in dark, older than in Fig. 167. (Reduced.)

we crush these stems with the fingers, we find those grown in the light firmer than those grown in the dark. A more accurate test would be to dry the plants thoroughly and then to weigh them. The plants grown in the light would outweigh those grown in the dark. In other words, they have made more plant substance. It will

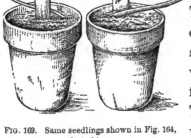

be remembered that green plants form starch in sunlight. The starch is used, much of it, in making new plant substance, especially cell walls, which constitute the firmer portions of plants. This is the reason, then, why the stems grown in the dark are more slender

FIG. 169. Same seedlings shown in Fig. 164, but older.

and less firm than those grown in the light.

The leaves on plants grown in the dark. While stems grow less rapidly in light than in dark, light accelerates the growth of the leaves. Plants grown in the dark have very small or undeveloped leaves. This is well shown in the pumpkin (Fig. 169). Compare the leaves on the plant grown in the dark with those on the plant grown in the light. The plants are of the same age.

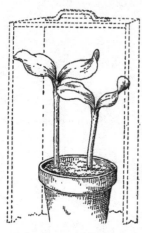

Light, then, increases the size of the leaves of such plants as the pumpkin, sunflower, buckwheat, etc. How is it with the wheat and similar plants?

Do the cotyledons of the pumpkin or squash open in the dark? As the cotyledons of the pumpkin slip from the seed coats and are pulled out of the ground by the loop, they are clasped tightly together. But as they are straightening up in the

Fig. 170. Sunflower seedlings grown in light, just covered to exclude light.

light they spread apart and expand. What causes them to open and expand? Let us cover some pumpkin seedlings which have grown in the light, and in which the cotyledons have just expanded. The box should be tight so that the seedlings will be kept in the dark. Allow them to remain here a day or two; then remove the box sometime near mid-day. The cotyledons are clasped together and erect, as in Fig. 171. Now leave them uncovered; the

Fig. 171. Same seedlings after being covered two days.

cotyledons open again. If we examine them at night when it is dark, we usually find them clasped together and erect. As the morning light comes on they open again. The light, then, must have an influence in spreading the cotyledons apart.

We should now refer to our observations on the squash seedlings, grown in the dark, or if we did not then observe the cotyledons, we should at once examine some seedlings of the pumpkin or squash, grown in the dark, as shown in Fig. 164. The cotyledons remain closed. Fig. 169 is very interesting; the stem as it grows is obliged to push its way

Fig. 172. Same seedlings after exposure to light again.

out from between the cotyledons at one side, so tightly are they clasped together. These cotyledons have never opened because they have been kept from the light.

Arrangement of leaves in relation to light. The position of the leaves on plants, whether the plant is small or large, is such as to place the leaf so that it will receive an abundance of light. The relation of the leaves of a given plant to one another is such as to give all the leaves an opportunity to receive light with the least possible interference. Plants of several different types in this respect may be brought into the class-room so that the pupils may make comparisons; although such observations should be made in fields and gardens whenever possible.

Influence of light on the day position of leaves. Light has great influence on the position of the leaves during

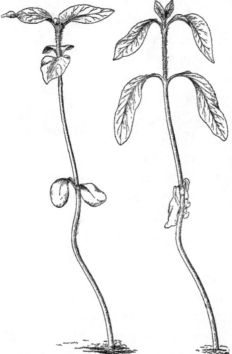

the day, just as it has on the position of the pumpkin cotyledons which we have just studied, or on the leaves of the sensitive plant. It acts as a stimulus to adjust the leaf so that the light will fall full upon the upper surface, or nearly so. In some plants this position becomes more or less fixed. But in other plants, like the sunflower, bean,

FIG. 173. Young sunflower plant; at left in light, at right after being covered two days to shut out light.

oxalis, and many more, the leaves change their position night and day. The leaves usually occupy a drooping position at night, and on the following morning they are brought by the influence of light into the day position again. This drooping position of leaves at night has been termed the "sleep of plants," but it is not in any sense a sleep. In the "compass" plant the leaves stand vertical and point north and south.

The night position of leaves is due to unequal growth. When the leaves are young and in the bud, they closely overlap one another. This is due to the fact that growth takes place more rapidly on the under surface of the young leaf. This causes the leaf to curve upward and in, over the end of the stem. But as the leaves become older, growth takes place more rapidly on the upper surface. This causes them to curve outward and later downward so that they occupy a drooping position. This can be demonstrated by covering for several

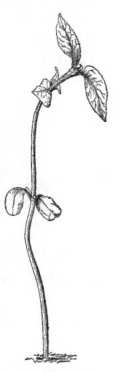

Fig. 174. Young sunflower. plant turned toward light from window.

days a bean plant, or by covering an oxalis plant for a day, so that it will be entirely in the dark.

To illustrate it here a sunflower plant grown in a pot was used, the plant being four or five weeks old.   It

was covered one day, and then at noon on the following day the box was lifted off. The leaves of the
sunflower were in the position shown in Fig. 173, the
right-hand plant. This shows that if the plant is in
darkness the leaves droop, and the drooping has nothing
to do with night time, except that the light stimulus is
then removed. When
the plant is exposed
to the light, the light
draws the leaf up into
the day position.

FIG. 175. Sunflower with young head turned
toward morning sun.

**The leaves of many
plants turn so as to
face the light.** From
some of the foregoing
studies we learn that
the leaves of plants
are sensitive to the
stimulus of light.
They stand so that the rays of light fall full upon the
upper surface. In the open, the leaves of many plants
stand so that the upper surface receives the light directly
from above, as the light from this direction in cloudy
days is strongest. The leaves of many other plants
change their positions through the day if the sun is
shining, so that their upper surfaces face the sun
directly, or nearly so, at all times of the day.

Turning of the sunflower plant toward the sun. During the period of growth of the sunflower plant the leaves, as well as the growing part of the stem, are very sensitive to light. On sunny days the leaves on the growing end of the stem are drawn somewhat together so that they form a rosette. They also turn so that the rosette faces the sun when it is rising.

FIG. 176. Same sunflower plant photographed just at sundown.

The growing part of the stem also turns toward the sun; this aids in bringing the upper surfaces of the leaves to face the sun. All through the day, if the sun continues to shine, the rosette of leaves follows it, and at sundown the rosette faces squarely

FIG. 177. Same plant a little older when the head does not turn, but the stem and leaves do.

the western horizon. For a week or more the sunflower head will face the sun directly and follow it all day as surely as does the rosette of

FIG. 178. The young head follows the sun even though the leaves are cut away.

leaves. At length, a little while before the flowers in the head blossom, the head ceases to turn, but the rosette of leaves and the stem also, to some extent, continue to turn with the sun. When the leaves become mature and cease growing, they also cease to turn. It is not true that the fully opened sunflower head turns with the sun, as is commonly supposed. But I have observed young heads four to five

FIG. 179. Seedling sunflower; at left with light from above, at right turned toward window.

inches in diameter follow the sun all day. The growing end of the stem will also follow the sun, even if all the leaves and the young flower head are cut away.

Experiments with sunflowers and other seedlings. The seedlings of many plants are so sensitive to the influence of light that they quickly turn if placed near a window where there is a one-sided

illumination. The pot of seedlings shown in Fig. 180 was placed near a window. In an hour they had turned so that the cotyledons faced the light coming in from the window. Even when

FIG. 180. Sunflower seedlings lighted from above.

FIG. 181. Same seedlings by a window.

the cotyledons are cut off, the stems will turn toward the light, as shown in Fig. 182. Any of the seedlings which we have studied, or others, will turn to one side where there is a one-sided illumination, but some will turn more quickly than others.

The influences which light has on the position of leaves, on the growth of the stem, and on the symmetrical or one-sided growth of the branches of a tree, can be seen and observed in any place

FIG. 182. The seedlings turn, even though the cotyledons are cut away, and stem is cut in two.

where plants grow. It will be interesting then, when you come in the presence of plants, for you to endeavor to read from the plants themselves the varied stories which they can tell of the influence which light has on them. Where leaves are crowded together, you will often see that each leaf in the cluster takes a definite place, so that it will be in a good position to get the light. This position of the leaf is not taken of itself alone. It is because the light, acting on it, causes it to take up this position. Leaves thus often form what are called pieces of " mosaic,"

FIG. 183. Cedar of Lebanon, strong light only from one side of tree (Syria).

as seen in the Fittonia (Fig. 102) cultivated in green-houses. In the woods or groves you will have an opportunity of studying many of these " mosaics," and it will be interesting for you to see if there is any difference in the size of any part of the leaf which enables it better to take a favorable position in the

" mosaic."   Then on the edge of the forest or grove you can study many examples of the effect of light on the unequal growth of the branches of trees and shrubs.

What advantage to the plant comes from this power to turn the leaves so as to face the light ?   What plant food can be formed only in the green leaves in the

FIG. 184.   Spray of leaves of striped maple, showing different lengths of leafstalks.

presence of light ?   What economy is there in the plants' having broad and thin leaves, instead of having the same amount of tissue in a rounded green mass ? Why do trees on the edge of a forest, or of a grove, have more and longer branches on the side away from other trees than on the side next the forest ?   In leaf clusters on branches why are some of the leafstalks much longer than others (see Fig. 184)?

CHAPTER XXI

BEHAVIOR OF CLIMBING PLANTS

Different ways of getting up to the light. Plants have different ways of getting into a position where

Fig. 185. Coiling stem of morning-glory.

there is light. Trees build tall, stout trunks, which hold their branches and leaves far above other plants. Shrubs and tall herbs build slender trunks to get

above their smaller neighbors. Some other plants
which have comparatively weak stems have found
means of getting up where there is light. Such plants
climb. Their stems cannot hold the plants upright.
They climb on other plants, or on rocks,
fences, houses, etc.

**Climbing by coiled
stems.** A common
way for some plants
to climb is to coil or
twine their stems
round other plants.
The morning-glory,
the climbing bitter-
sweet or waxwork
(*celastrus*), and the
nightshade are
examples. While
these plants are

FIG. 186.   Coiling stem of dodder.

growing, watch the stems and see how they coil.
The young stems are more or less erect; but
the end of the stem is often bent to one side. You
may watch the plant in the field, or several shoots
may be cut and placed in a vessel of water. Notice
now which way the bent ends point. In an hour or
so look again. Some of them are pointing in a
different direction. If you look at intervals through

the day, you will see that the stem swings slowly
around in circles.

The nightshade swings from right to left, or "against
the sun." The morning-glory coils in the same direction. Which way does the climbing bittersweet coil? How is it with the "dodder,"
or "love vine"? Study other vines that
you see. If you wind the morning-glory
vine or the bittersweet in the opposite way
from that in which you find it growing,
and fasten it, which way will the young
end coil when left to itself?

FIG. 187. Stem of
dodder with
suckers entering
the stem of its
victim.

Climbing by tendrils. The pea vine,
the star cucumber, and some other plants
climb by tendrils. The
squash, pumpkin, cucum-
bers, and melons also have
tendrils, but rarely climb,
as they are usually cultivated where
there is no opportunity. But these
plants are good ones for the study of
tendrils, as they grasp other plants near
them. Their tendrils are long and slender. Before they have caught hold of
a support the end is curved to one side
and the tendril swings, somewhat as the stem of the
morning-glory does, until it touches some object. The

FIG. 188. Coiling ten-
dril of bryony.

end of the tendril now coils round the object if it is not too large. If you watch a tendril from day to day after it has caught hold, you will see that it finally curls up into a beautiful coiled spring. Consult Fig. 122 to see how you can imitate the action of a tendril with a strip of dandelion stem.

Tendrils often grasp the edge of a leaf and coil on both sides of the leaf. The tendrils of the star cucumber do this frequently. The end of the tendril can take hold of the flat surface of a leaf and hold on by tiny suckers

FIG. 189.   Tendril of star cucumber grasping edge of leaf of nightshade.

or root-like processes, which it sends out to penetrate the leaf. These suckers grow out from the surface of the coiled tendril and strike into the object much as the suckers of the dodder strike into its host.

The Japanese ivy, or Boston ivy, as it is sometimes called, climbs by tendrils.   It is often used to train on the walls of houses.   Where the ends of the tendrils strike against the hard wall of the house, they flatten out into little disks, which cling very firmly and hold up the large and heavy vines.

The clematis, or virgin's bower, climbs in a peculiar way. The petiole, or midrib of the leaf, acts like a

FIG. 190.   Tendril of Japanese ivy.

tendril and coils round an object for support.

Root climbers.   Poison ivy is a plant which some persons should avoid.   Others can handle it without becoming poisoned.   One form of the plant grows in the shape of a vine which climbs up the trunks of tall trees.   It may be known from other vines in the woods by the shape of its leaves.   But especially can one tell it in the woods by the numerous climbing roots which cover the side toward the tree, and which take hold in crevices in the bark and hold the vine up.   There is a

FIG. 191.   Vine of *ampelopsis* (American creeper) clambering over a dead tree trunk.

shrubby form of poison ivy which does not climb. One should learn to know the plant by the leaves. See Fig. 84.

The climbing poison ivy sometimes forms a very large vine, which reaches to the top of tall trees and nearly smothers them with its dense foliage. The English ivy, sometimes trained on the sides of houses, is a root climber.

Some plants climb by leaning on others for support. As they grow upward, being too weak to support themselves alone, they fall against other plants and grow over and between their branches. Such plants are sometimes called *scramblers,* because they scramble over others.

CHAPTER XXII

THE BEHAVIOR OF FLOWERS

THE BUTTERCUP FLOWER

Buttercups. Before we read stories on the behavior of flowers we must know the parts of the flower. This is because the different parts of the flower have different kinds of work to do, and therefore behave differently. Buttercups, no doubt, are known to all who have been in the fields and woods in the spring.

The petals. The bright yellow parts which give the cup shape and the yellow color to the flower are *petals*,

FIG. 192. Flower of buttercup, sepals below, petals next, then stamens and pistils in center.

as perhaps all of you know. There are usually five of these petals. All together they are called the *corolla*.

The sepals. When you have removed the petals you will see, just below where they were seated, a crown of small scale-like bodies. Each one of these is a *sepal*. There are usually five of these, and together they are called the *calyx*.

The stamens and pistils. If you look now at the remaining parts of the flower, you will see that there

156

are two kinds. Next to the petals are a goodly number of small stalked bodies called *stamens.* If the little cases on the ends of the stalks have not already opened, prick one open with a pin. The cases crack open of themselves, and a yellow dust-like powder comes out. This is *pollen,* each tiny dust-like particle being a *pollen grain.* The cases on the ends of the stalks are *pollen cases.* Right in the center of the flower are a number of stouter bodies which have tapering points. These are called *pistils.*

What the parts of the flower do. If you look at the young flower bud, you will see that the parts are all wrapped up snugly and covered over by the sepals. The work of the sepals here is to protect the other parts of the flower while they are young. The petals are bright colored, large, and showy. They are the parts of the flower which attract us. They attract bees and other insects. Did you ever see the bees visiting the flowers, going from one blossom to another? They reach down and lap up the bit of honey

FIG. 193. Seed, or akene, of buttercup.

that is in a claw-like pocket at the bottom of each petal. In doing this their legs drag on the pollen cases. The bees scatter the pollen grains all around as they visit one flower after another. As they crawl over the flowers some of the pollen clinging to the hairs on their legs is left on the pointed ends of the pistils.

Where the seed is formed. If you keep watch of some flowers day after day, you can read the story of where the seed is formed. You can read it all on the same day if you have plants on which are flowers of different ages. You should begin with the younger ones and read up through the older ones. You will read that the sepals fall away; the petals wither and fall ; the stamens wither, but the pistils grow larger. After a time they will ripen and you can find the seed. The story of just how the seed is formed is a hard one to read, and I am afraid it would be hard for you to understand if I should tell it. But I have attempted to tell it in Chapter XXV. I may tell you, though, that unless each part of the flower did its work faithfully, the seed could not be formed.

BEHAVIOR OF THE PUMPKIN FLOWER

The petals. If you cannot find a pumpkin flower, certainly you can see a squash flower in some garden. The story of the squash flower is very much like that of the pumpkin flower. I do not need to tell you that the flower is very different from that of the buttercup. You can see that. Where are the petals ? I believe you can read in the flower that the large, yellow, showy, urn-shaped part just inside the calyx is the corolla. How many points are there on

the rim of the urn-shaped corolla ?   Five, you say, and
you have read that each one of these represents a petal,
and that all the petals are joined together by their edges.

The sepals.   Below the corolla you see five green
pointed leaf-like parts arranged in the form of a crown.
What does each one of these parts represent ?

The stamens and pistils.   Now

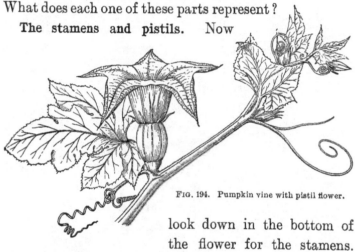

FIG. 194.   Pumpkin vine with pistil flower.

look down in the bottom of
the flower for the stamens.
All the flowers are not alike, you see.   There is a column
in the center of each.   On some of these there is pollen.
These columns in some of the flowers are different from
the columns in others.   Are the flowers all alike on the
outside ?   No!   Those with the three blunt projections
on the end of the column have a round enlargement on
the flower stalk.   In the other flowers there is no
enlargement on the flower stalk, and the column of
these bears pollen grains.   So these columns must be

stamens joined together. The columns in the others
form the upper part of the pistils joined together, while
the enlargement in the flower stalk is
the lower part of the joined pistils.
The point on the pistil where the pollen lodges we call the *stigma.*

FIG. 195. Stamen
flower closed.

Bees and other insects go from one
flower to another.   How otherwise
could the pollen be taken from the
stamen flower and be placed on the
end of the pistil in the pistil flower?
So the bees are a great help to the
flower in making its seed, and the
flower gives the bee honey to pay for
its labor. If you
can get a pumpkin
in the autumn, cut
one in two, cross-
wise. You see what
a great number of
seeds there are. Can
you tell how many
parts are joined in
this compound pistil
which finally makes
the pumpkin?

FIG. 196. Stamen-
flower front cut
a w a y, showing
stamens grown
together in cen-
ter.

FIG. 197. Pistil flower with
front cut away.

THE SUNFLOWER

The flower head. We have already seen how the sunflower plant behaves toward light. We are now interested in observing the behavior of the flowers. You should learn, first of all, that the large, showy blos-

FIG. 198. Squash vine with flowers and young squash.

som is not a single flower. It is made up of a great many flowers. It is a "head" of flowers. There are two kinds of flowers in a head. I am sure you can tell the two kinds apart. The most showy ones are on the edge or margin of the head. They stand out like rays of the sun; so we call them *ray flowers*. The

most prominent part is like a strap.   The other flowers
are more numerous.   They are shaped somewhat like a
tube, and have been called *tubular flowers*.   Because
they form a large disk in the center of the flower head
they are also called *disk flowers*.   Each one of the little
ray and disk flowers
is called a *floret*.

FIG. 199. Sunflower head.

**The behavior of the
florets in flowering.**
If you will read from
several sunflower
heads, or read from
one day by day, you
will learn an interest-
ing story. You can
cut off a head and
put the stem in a
vessel of water in the
room where you can see it from day to day. It will
behave very well for several days. You do not need
to pick the flowers to pieces. Just look now and then
at the disk florets.

First, in those next the ray flowers, the pollen is
pushed out from the pollen cases and lifted above the
corolla tube, so that the pollen grains can be scattered.
It is the growing pistil in each floret which pushes the
pollen out.   Then in a few more rings next these and

nearer the center the same thing happens ; and so on toward the center of the disk, each day the ring of opening florets approaching nearer the center.   Finally the pistil pushes up its style so that it stands above the end of the corolla tube.   The style is divided into two slender parts which at first are closed up so the pollen cannot touch the stigma on the inner surface.   Later

FIG. 200.   Heads of fuller's teasel in different stages of flowering.

the parts curve outward.   When the head has partly blossomed you can see a broad ring of disk flowers, next the rays, with the pistils projecting above the corolla tube.   Next there is a broad ring of disk flowers with the pollen projecting above the corolla tube, and in the center of the head are disk flowers not yet opened.

If you observe the flowers in the garden, you will see that bees and other insects are crawling over them.

The bees drag the pollen from the open florets where the pistil is closed to the open pistils. Since the pistils and stamens of each floret do not ripen at the same time, the pollen from one floret must go to the pistil of another floret, and cannot get to its own. This is a good thing for the plant, for it makes the new life

FIG. 201. A group of jacks.

FIG. 202. Jack in his pulpit.

in the seed more vigorous. This taking of the pollen from one flower to another is *cross pollination*. If you study the behavior of flowers in this respect, you will find that insects visit a great many different kinds and cross pollinate them.

If you find a daisy, golden-rod, aster, or black-eyed Susan, read it to see how it compares with the sunflower.

The Teasel

The behavior of the teasel in flowering. Do you know the teasel? It is worth your while to learn where it grows, that you may see its interesting way of flowering. The

FIG. 203. Jack out of his pulpit: the two upper ones with pistil flowers, the two lower ones with stamen flowers.

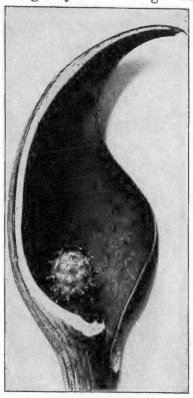

FIG. 204. Flower of skunk cabbage with front cut away.

plant grows in waste places, along roadsides, and in some places is cultivated as

fuller's teasel. The flowers are in heads. I am going to
show you a photograph of several heads, with the blos-

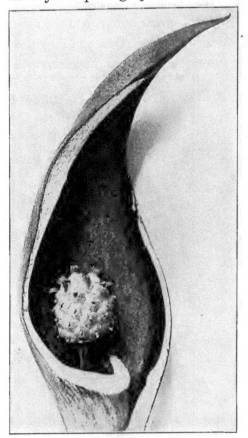

soming of the
plants in differ-
ent stages and let
you read the sto-
ry (see Fig. 200).

**Jack-in-the-
pulpit flower.**
You are all in-
terested in the
Jack-in-the-
pulpit. The
" jack " is tall,
and his head
reaches up so
that we can see
it in the pulpit.
If you examine
them, you will
see that some
jacks are covered
below with sta-
men flowers,
while other jacks

FIG. 205. Another flower of skunk cabbage.

are covered below with pistil flowers. How does the
pollen get from one jack to the other (Figs. 201–203)?

The skunk cabbage.   In this plant the stamens and pistils are both in the same flower.   Can you read their story (Figs. 204, 205) ?

The wind helps to cross pollinate many flowers.   In many plants no provision is made for using insects to carry the pollen.   For many of these plants the wind carries the pollen.   The oak, corn, wheat, grasses, etc., are examples of wind-pollinated flowers.

CHAPTER XXIII

HOW FRUITS ARE FORMED

The fruit contrasted with the seed. The fruit comes after the flower. As the fruit ripens, the seed matures. Is the fruit the same as the seed? In Fig. 25 is shown a fruit of the sunflower. It is usually called a seed. It is formed from a single flower in the head. Since there are many flowers in a sunflower head, there are also many fruits. The entire fruit, however, is not, strictly speaking, the seed. The seed is inside. The wall of the seed is so firmly joined to the wall of the pistil that it does not separate from it, and the meat (embryo plant) is inside. So we cannot say with accuracy that the fruit and seed are the same.[1]

NOTE. — The matter of this chapter is not particularly concerned with the behavior of plants. But the fruit is best studied after the flower, if we wish to get any idea of the parts entering into the fruit. Its study is also closely connected with the dispersal of seed. For this reason the chapter on fruits is introduced here. If the teacher prefers, the matter of the flower, fruit, and of seed dispersal may quite as well be introduced after Chapter X, in connection with a study of the plant and its parts.

[1] In the gingko tree, and in cycas, the fruit is the same as the seed, though sometimes the embryo is not formed in the fruit. The word "fruit" has a very indefinite significance, as can be seen from its

The a-kene'. The seed or fruit of the sunflower is called an *a-kene'*. The beggar needles, seeds of the golden-rod, etc., are also akenes. In the buttercup it

is difficult for us to say just what is the fruit. The collection of seeds in the ripe or old flower is probably a fruit, since they are all formed from a single flower. Each part, however, is an akene (Fig. 210) and is generally called a seed, though the wall of the seed is united with the wall of the pistil. An akene, then, is a dry unopening fruit, with a single seed the wall of which is joined with the

FIG. 206. An akene or fruit of sunflower with four embryos in one seed coat, germinating.

wall of the pistil.

The pod. The pea pod is a good example of one kind of fruit. It is a capsule fruit which has only one chamber, or *loc-ule*. It opens into halves by splitting along the two edges. You can see the seeds inside, and that they are attached at one point to the wall of the pod. The silkweed or milkweed has a fruit which

FIG. 207. An older stage of Fig. 206.

general application to widely different structures or combinations. We even speak of the fruit of ferns, meaning the spore cases and spores, where no seeds at all are formed.

is an example of another kind of pod, which opens only
along one edge.   The morning-glory has a pod, or capsule fruit, with three chambers or locules,
each one representing a part of the pistil.
Can you name and describe
other pods ?   How should you
describe a pod or
capsule fruit ?

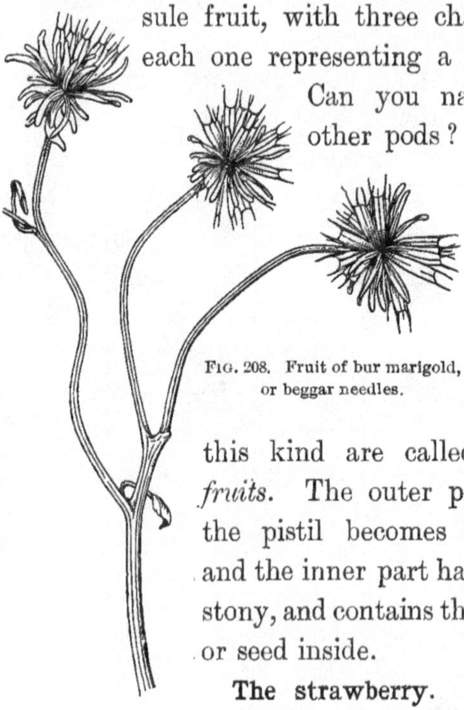

**Drupes or stone
fruits.**   The
cherry, peach,

FIG. 208.   Fruit of bur marigold,
or beggar needles.

plum, and other
fleshy fruits of
this kind are called *drupes* or *stone
fruits*.   The outer part of the wall of
the pistil becomes fleshy,
and the inner part hard and
stony, and contains the meat
or seed inside.

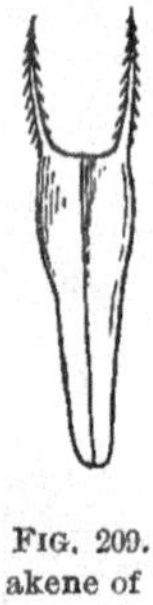

The strawberry.   When
you next have some berries you will find it
interesting to learn what parts of the flower
make the edible portion of the fruit.   In the
strawberry you can see the tiny
seeds, each resting in a tiny de-
pression, as if they were stuck all over
the outer part of the pulp or soft part of

FIG. 209.
An akene of bur
marigold, the
" bootjack."

FIG. 210. Akene
of buttercup.

the strawberry. They are not covered with any soft
substance. Each seed is a ripened pistil. There were
many pistils in the strawberry flower. If
you go into a strawberry patch when the

FIG. 211. Fruit of
pea: a pod split
open.

berries are
ripening,
you can see
how the
fleshy part
of the
strawberry
is formed, by reading
the stories from the
flower through the
green strawberries up
to the ripe ones. You
will see that the part of
the flower to which the
pistils are joined grows
larger and thicker, and
finally forms the fleshy
part of the strawberry,
raising the seeds up as
it grows bigger. This
part of a flower, to

FIG. 212. Pods of milkweed.

which the pistils and usually the other parts are joined,
is called the *re-cep'ta-cle* or *to'rus*. *The fleshy part of*

the strawberry, then, is the **receptacle.** The strawberry
is not, strictly speaking, a berry. *A berry is a fleshy
fruit with several seeds inside,* as
the snowberry, gooseberry, grape,
tomato, etc.

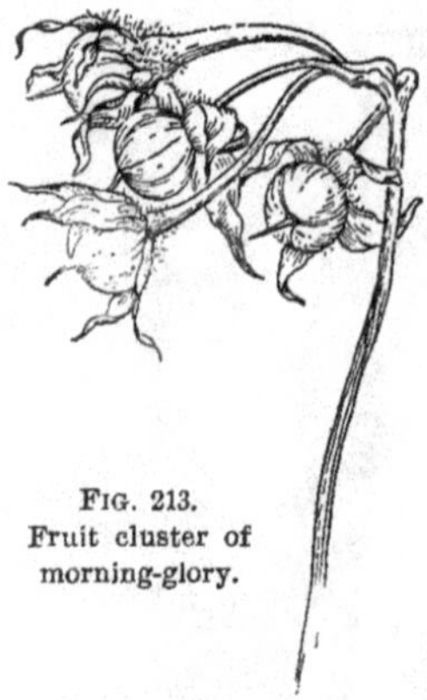

The blackberry. How is it with
the blackberry fruit? You can
read the story in the same way as
you did in the strawberry, when
you have a chance. The receptacle
becomes larger and longer, and
forms the inside of the blackberry
which we eat, though it is not a
very juicy part. Where are the seeds? They are
enclosed in a fleshy substance. This fleshy substance
around each seed is the outside of the pistil. How
different it is from the strawberry!

FIG. 213.
Fruit cluster of
morning-glory.

The raspberry. Compare the raspberry fruit with that of the strawberry
and blackberry. Read the story and
see if you can tell what part of the
flower makes the fruit. You should go
to a raspberry patch, or have some stems with ripe
raspberries and, if possible, flowers on them.

FIG. 214. Single pod
with three locules
of morning-glory.

*The raspberry and blackberry are not, strictly speaking,
berries. They are collections of tiny stone fruits.* In
the flowers the pistils are separate, but as the fruit

forms, the outer fleshy parts unite to form a collection of little drupes.

The apple is an interesting fruit. It would be difficult for you to read the entire story, because older students

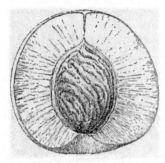

are not sure that they know just what parts are united in the apple fruit. Cut an apple crosswise. You see the seeds inside. How many chambers, or locules, are there for seeds? What does each one of these locules represent? I shall not ask you what the fleshy part of the apple represents, for we

FIG. 215. Drupe or stone fruit of peach.

are not sure that we know. It was once thought to be the calyx grown very thick and fleshy. You see at the small end of the apple the dried ends of the sepals.

But perhaps these sepals only rested on the edge of the receptacle which is joined to the outer part of the compound pistil. If this is so, then the receptacle grows very large and fleshy and forms the fleshy part of

FIG. 216. Fruit of strawberry and raspberry.

the apple. This is most likely. Compare the receptacle of the rose flower. The rose flower is a near relative

of the apple flower, and we should expect the flowers
to be somewhat alike, though not entirely so.   An apple
fruit is sometimes called a *pome.*   If you will compare
it with the true berries, like the snowberry, gooseberry,
etc., you will see that it is very much like a berry.

The squash, pumpkin, cucumber, and other fruits of
this kind form what is called a *pepo.*   The outer part
is supposed to be formed from the receptacle of the
flower which here is united with the three parts of
the compound pistil.   You will remember that in the
flower (Fig. 194) the calyx and corolla were seated on
the end of the young pumpkin, which suggests that
the receptacle here encloses and is joined to the
pistil.   How many chambers, or locules, are there in
the pumpkin?

Acorn fruits.   The fruit of the oaks is interesting to
us all.   Every one knows the acorns and the cups in
which they rest.   Well, the cup is a very singular part
of the fruit.   It perhaps represents a crown of tiny
leaves around the base of the young flower.   As the
acorn was forming, these tiny leaves grew larger and
were all joined closely together, so that they formed a
cup which partly enclosed the acorn (see Fig. 245).

In the hazelnut, chestnut, and beechnut a similar
crown of leaves (*in-vo-lu'cre*) around the base of the
flower forms the husk or bur in which the nuts are
enclosed, and from which they are shelled when ripe.

There are many other fruits which will be interesting to study. Some of these are treated of in the following chapter, since in many cases it is difficult to distinguish between a fruit and a seed. In the study of fruits you should see if you can tell of what use they are to the plant, and how these fruits may be the means of helping the plants to scatter their seeds.

NOTE. — In the walnut, butternut, and hickory nut the fruit is different from that of the hazelnuts, oaks, etc. The "hull" or "shuck" probably consists partly of calyx and partly of involucral bracts consolidated, but very likely there is more of calyx than of involucre. The walnut and butternut are more often called drupes or stone fruits, but the fleshy part of the fruit is evidently not of the same origin as in the case of the true drupes, like the cherry, peach, plum, and others.

CHAPTER XXIV

HOW PLANTS SCATTER THEIR SEED

The **touch-me-not.** Did you ever see or handle a pod of a "touch-me-not"? The plant is sometimes known

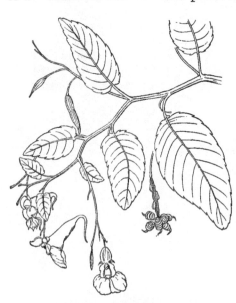

as garden balsam. It is well worth while to grow it in any flower garden. The flowers are pretty, but the pods are still more interesting. When you touch them, or throw them on the floor or against the wall, they burst suddenly and scatter their seeds all around. The wild *Impatiens*, or jewel

FIG. 217. Spray of leaves and flowers and fruit of jewel weed, or wild *Impatiens*.

weed, has smaller pods, which burst in the same way. Find some of the plants in a garden during the autumn and try the pods, or look for the wild *Impatiens*, or jewel weed, along streams and in damp, shady places.

The witch hazel. The witch hazel is known by its beautiful yellow flowers with slender curled petals, which come out late in autumn, after the leaves have fallen. At the same time the fruit pods are matured from flowers of the previous year. On dry days, when the fruit is ripe, one can hear the snapping of the pods as they burst, and the seeds are thrown with force several feet away. Pods which

FIG. 218.   Seeds of milkweed ready to scatter from the pods.

burst and scatter their seeds are called *explosive fruits.* Other examples are to be found in the vetch, locust, violet, oxalis, etc.

The milkweed or silkweed. The milkweed is known by its peculiar flowers and the abundance of white milky substance which flows from wounds in the plant, and gives a disagreeable sticky feeling to the hands when it comes in contact with them. When the flowers go, a few little boat-shaped pods are seen on the flower

stalk. These grow larger and larger. When they are
ripe the pods split open. A great mass of flat seeds is
crowded out by the pushing of great tufts of white
silky threads attached to one end of each seed. They
are so light and feathery that the wind lifts them
easily and sometimes bears them miles away.

Did you ever see these pods bursting and emptying
out the great white feathery cloud? Take a pod
before it has opened. Split it open and see how
beautifully the seeds are packed away in it. Separate
some of the seeds to see the soft, silky tuft of hairs
on the end. Blow the seeds into the air to see how
easily they float away on the "wings of the wind."

The dandelion. The dandelion is so common that
few persons admire the really beautiful flower. They
would rather get rid of it. If the dandelion would
only grow in out-of-the-way places, it would not be so
unwelcome. But it is an intruder. You dig the
plants, root and branch, out of your yard, and in a
few years they are there again, or new ones, rather.
It makes a great many seeds. But how beautifully
they sail through the air like tiny balloons!

Did you ever try to blow all the seeds off the head
with one long whiff? There is a mark left where each
one stood. How they go sailing away! Watch them!
Some are coming down to the ground like a man
clinging to a parachute. The seed is the heaviest part

and is below. On the end of the long stalk above is
the crown of soft white hairs which forms the float.
Down, down, the seed slowly comes and soon is ready

FIG. 219. Dandelion seeds.

to wriggle its way into the ground. Here it germinates and makes a new dandelion in the lawn.

The leaves form a deep-green rosette resting on the
grass. The flower stem comes up, and the flower head

FIG. 220. Dandelion fruit in shade (after Macmillan).

opens, showing a beautiful cluster of yellow flowers.
This head closes at night and opens in the day, closes
again at night and opens
with the day, and so on,
unless the day is a dark
one, when all the dande-
lions may remain closed.

By and by the head
stops opening. We can
see the tips of the flowers.
They wither and die. A
white cottony mass be-
gins to appear. Its silky
hairs spread apart, the
head opens again, and
the crown of narrow
leaves (the *involucre*) re-
curves and gives room
for the spreading crown
on the tips of all the
seeds. This forms a
great white ball on the

Fig. 221. Dandelion flower and fruit. Flower
open at right, old flowers closed and stems
elongating at left, ripe seed raised up higher
and ready to scatter (after Miyake).

end of the stem. The seeds are now in a position
where the wind easily catches them.

Did you ever notice that where the lawn is mowed
many of the dandelions have such short stems that
the flower head is below the lawn mower? Then see

how these same short stems will grow much longer just as the seeds are ready to be scattered, so that they are lifted above the grass where the wind may catch hold of them easily. Put a stake by some flowers and measure the stems. Then measure them every day while the seeds are ripening. Along the roadsides or in undisturbed places the flower stems are often longer than those on the lawn. Do these long stems lengthen as the seeds ripen?

The wild lettuce and prickly lettuce, so common in old fields and along the roadsides, have seeds very much like those of the dandelion.

The virgin's bower, or clematis. The clematis, or virgin's bower, is quite as attractive in appearance in the autumn as in the summer when it is in flower. The great masses of foliage and vines clambering over fences and shrubs, and often hiding them entirely, show numerous white puffs of feathery seeds where the flower once was. Each of the seeds is like an arrow-headed plume. Blow or scatter some of them to the wind and see them scudding off to the ground in curious spiral courses.

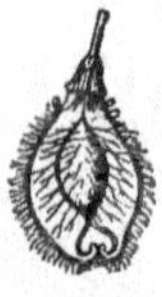

FIG. 222. Fruit (seed) of elm, a samara.

Winged seeds. Some seeds have wing-like expansions on the side and are called *winged seeds.* They, too, are carried by the wind, but they are not quite so buoyant as the seeds of the

milkweed and dandelion. The elm seed has two wings.
It is sometimes called a *samara*, which means "seed of
the elm." The maples and pines also have winged
seeds. Do you know any other plants
which have winged seeds?

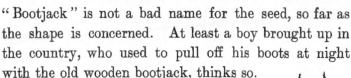

FIG. 223.
Winged fruit of maple,
two seeds.

The bur marigold. The bur marigold,
sometimes called "beggar needles" or
"devil's bootjack," is a very common
weed with yellow flower heads. The
seeds are also in a head, and the cluster
bristles all over with the barbed awns.
"Bootjack" is not a bad name for the seed, so far as
the shape is concerned. At least a boy brought up in
the country, who used to pull off his boots at night
with the old wooden bootjack, thinks so.

When tramping through the fields, or
sometimes in the garden, if you brush
against one of these plants, the awns will
pierce your clothing immediately. The
barbs hold on tight, and soon there may
be hundreds of these seeds clinging to you.

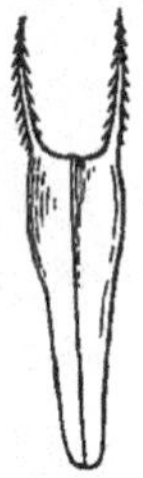

FIG. 224. Seed of
bur marigold,
"bootjack."

The cocklebur, burdock, stick-tights, etc.
The bur marigold is not the only seed or
fruit ready to "catch on" for a "free ride." There
are also cocklebur, burdock, stick-tight, and "what-
not," and it does not help matters to "crack behind,"
either. They hold on until they are pulled off, and

then they leave in the cloth countless tiny hooks, which are even harder to remove.

If you wish to know more about these " dead-beats " who ride all over the country and never pay a cent of fare, go out for a tramp in the autumn in old neglected

fields or in low waste ground. You can carry some home for study. Examine them to see the different kinds of seeds, and how the barbs, hooks, and other hold-fasts are formed. What animals do you think would be of service to the plant in dispersing such seeds? You may wish, also, to visit the same places in summer to see the plants in flower.

FIG. 223. Fruit of cocklebur with booked appendages.

Have you seen any other seeds than these described here which have means for dispersal? Do seeds ever float on the water and become scattered in this way? How is it with the cocoanut palm? Do seeds of grasses or weeds float in the water of lakes, ponds, rivers, and small streams?

PART IV

LIFE STORIES OF PLANTS

CHAPTER XXV

LIFE STORY OF THE SWEET PEA

THE life story of the sweet pea can be easily read from the plant by any one who wishes to grow it, and observe it. The story of the garden pea is similar, and some of you may wish to read it. But the sweet pea has prettier flowers. It can be grown in the garden, or in the plant house, or in the window garden where you can see it every day.

The seedling stage. The seeds of the sweet pea are round, hard, dark grayish brown objects (see Fig. 211). We plant them in the moist soil. They take water from the soil, swell up, and become soft. This moisture and the warmth in the soil start the dormant life in the seed into action. It "awakens," as we say, from its long sleep. In a few days, or a week or so, the young plant rises through the soil. The leaves are now tiny, but as the stem grows and the light has full

185

play on the small leaves they stretch out so that a
greater surface may receive light, for light is good for
the leaf and plant. As the stem gets longer, the leaves
higher up are better formed and more fully developed.

The growth and work period. If there are no sticks

FIG. 226. Sweet pea coming up.

or objects for the pea
vine to take hold of, it
will show you that it
needs some means of
support. It will soon
lie prostrate. But if
you put an upright
stick within its reach,
or train some cord or
string near by, the
tendrils on the leaf will
stretch out and coil
round it. In this way
the vine can climb up
where there is more
light and air. The
stem branches, and at length a tall and bushy plant is
formed. There is a much greater leaf surface.

While the plant has been growing, and lifting up
water and food from the soil by the combined work of
the roots and leaves and stem, the green leaves have
been doing another kind of work, for which we know

they need the help of sunlight. They have been making
starch. At night the starch is digested and changes to
sugar. It flows to all parts of the plant where growth
is taking place and new plant substance is wanted.
We know that if the pea vine were grown in the dark,
all the plant sub-
stance it would
have to use in
growth would be
that which was al-
ready in the seed.
The stem would be
for a time long
and spindling, the
leaves would be
small and yellow-
ish, and the frame-
work of the plant
would be soft. It

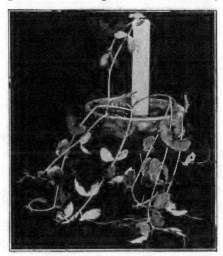

FIG. 227. Sweet-pea vines needing support.

would soon die. But in the light the leaves are green.
We know that the carbon dioxid of the air gets into
the green leaf. The light then helps the leaf to make
the starch from which most of the new plant substance
comes.

Flowering time. The plant has now formed a strong
working system, and its numerous branches bear many
working leaves. It is prepared to flower. Since the

flowers do another sort of work than make food, there
must be a good force of working leaves to supply the

FIG. 228. Sweet-pea vine trained to support.

food and energy needed in flowering. These appear
first, next come the flower heads, and later the clusters
of flowers, the older ones opening out first.

The Flower

The petals. The flower of the sweet pea is beautiful in color and form. Its form is peculiar; that is, it is not so regular in shape as the flower of the lily. Some one has thought the shape of the flower of the pea, and of its cousins or relations, to be like that of a butterfly. The most attractive parts of the flower of the pea are the petals. I think you already know what petals are. If you do not, just look at the pea flower, select the bright-colored parts which are thin and broad. These are the petals. You see they are of different shapes, instead of having the same shape as in the lily or

Fig. 229.   Sweet-pea flowers and young pods.

buttercup. This is what gives the peculiar form to the pea flower.

Now all these parts, or the different kinds of petals of the pea flower, have received names. I should not be surprised if, after studying their shapes carefully and their position in the flower, you could name them

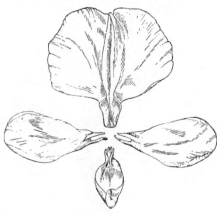

yourself, especially if you tried to think of things with which you are familiar and which these petals resemble.

Now, first, the large one, held up above, is the *banner*. The two reaching out on the sides are *wings*. Now think

Fig. 230. Petals of sweet pea.

hard for the two below, folded up together. Did you ever make or sail a boat? What does the boat have on the underside that cuts through the water? The *keel*. *Banner, wings, keel,* — these are the petals of the pea flower and all together we call them the *corolla*.

Now remove the petals from the flower. Place them out in position and draw the form. The two parts which form the keel are joined in the middle. Is that the case with the keel in the garden pea?

The calyx. The petals are removed from the flower ; what remains? Just below where they were joined there is a little crown of five pointed green leaf-like bodies. They are very different in form from the real pea leaves, but like them are green. These are *sepals*. Together they make the *calyx*. In the bud they covered and protected the other parts of the flower. There are five sepals, the same number as the petals, yet they are very different in form and color.

The stamens and pistil. There are now remaining the parts of the flower around which the keel was folded. Count them. There are ten thread-like bodies, surrounding a tiny boat-shaped body. The thread-like bodies are the stamens.

FIG. 231. Flower of sweet pea with petals removed.

Each one has an enlargement at the curved end. It is a little case containing the powder-like substance, called *pollen*. It is a *pollen case*. See if all the stamens are separate down to the calyx. One is. The nine others are joined toward the base. These nine form *one brotherhood*. The other one is a brotherhood all by itself. The pistil is flat, like a thin boat, and it is hairy. It is almost too tiny in the fresh flower for us to study. We will take one in an older flower.

The old flower. As the flower gets old the petals and stamens wither and die. They either fall away or collapse around the pistil. If the flower has done the work for which it was intended, the pistil does not die. It grows longer and broader and thicker, until we see that it is becoming a pea pod. When it has grown a

little, split the young pod open into halves, the same way that you have seen peas or beans shelled. Attached to one edge of the inside of the little pod you will see tiny roundish bodies, in the position in which you find the peas or seeds in the older pods. The pod is a sort of box which contains the seeds. The tiny bodies are cases in which the embryos are formed. They may be called *embryo cases* then. The case and embryo together make the seed. The pistil, or seed box, contains embryo cases in which seeds are formed.

FIG. 232. Fruit of sweet pea.

How the seed is formed. You cannot see how the seed is formed. This part of the story has been found out by those who are accustomed to use a powerful microscope. They cut up the growing embryo case (ovule) into very thin layers and search in these with a microscope to see the work that is done here. Thus we read the story of how the seed is formed.

In the first place there is a royal bit of life substance in the very young embryo case, known as the *germ* or *egg*. When the pollen is scattered from the pollen cases some of it falls on the end of the pistil. The pollen grain then starts to grow. It forms a slender tube as fine as a spider's silk. This pollen tube grows down through the pistil, and one enters each embryo case. In each pollen tube there are two bits of royal life substance, called *sperms*.

One sperm escapes from the pollen tube when it has entered the young embryo case and unites with the germ. *The union of these two bits of royal life substance, the sperm and germ, gives a new life to the germ and a new impetus for growth to the embryo case.* The new germ grows to form the embryo plant in the seed, while the new growth of the embryo case around it makes the seed coat. The pea seed is then formed. This completes the life story of the pea.

CHAPTER XXVI

LIFE STORY OF THE OAK

The white oak. In the autumn, when the leaves begin to fall, the acorns fall, too, from the oaks. They nestle in the grass or roll down into the furrow or ditch, or strike on the leaf floor of the forest, according to where the tree happens to be. The rains beat on the soil, and some of the acorns become partly buried in the ground. Some are eaten by insects, others are carried away by squirrels and other animals. Some are left to grow.

Fig. 233. White oak in autumn.

As we have seen in our study of the germination of the acorn, the root and stem parts of the embryo back out of the shell at the pointed end. The great fleshy cotyledons remain inside. The root pushes its way further down into the ground. The young stem grows out from between the cotyledon stalks. This often begins in the autumn. It continues in the spring among those seedlings which survive the

cold of the winter. Or, if the acorn did not germinate
in the autumn, it may in the spring. During the first
few years the tiny
oak makes little
growth. A few
leaves on a slender
stem appear. It is
not high enough to
be seen above the grass. Of the many which
start, but few rise up to saplings. Many, many years
the oak grows. It gets a foot or so higher each year.
It is making root, trunk, branches, and each year a

FIG. 234. Germinating acorn of
white oak.

FIG. 235. Oak trees getting a start. (Photographed in winter.)

greater number of leaves. The leaves make the
plant substance for the new and continued growth.

The bark on the trunk is smooth at
first. As the sapling gets older the
bark begins to crack open in long and
irregular fissures, making the gray bark

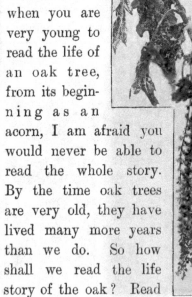

more promi-
nent. If you
should start
when you are
very young to
read the life of
an oak tree,
from its begin-
ning as an
acorn, I am afraid you
would never be able to
read the whole story.
By the time oak trees
are very old, they have
lived many more years
than we do. So how
shall we read the life
story of the oak? Read

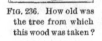

Fig. 236. How old was
the tree from which
this wood was taken?

it in a large number of trees, from Fig. 237. Scarlet oak,
spray of leaves and
young ones to middle-aged ones, and stamen clusters.

very old oaks. If you happen to find an oak tree which has been cut down, you know you can tell its age within a few years by counting the annual rings. During the first few years of the seedling, so little growth in diameter took place each year that the rings are not well marked.

FIG. 238. Spray of leaves and flowers of red oak, pistil flowers small above, stamen flowers in long clusters.

The oak flower. It is many years before the oak comes to flower. Not until it has become quite a tree are the flowers seen. They appear in the early spring, before the leaves show themselves. Have you seen the long, slender, graceful clusters hanging on the

FIG. 239.
Stamen flower
of red oak.

FIG. 240.
Pistil flower of
red oak.

branches of the middle-aged or old oak in the spring, when the limbs are yet bare? Gather some of these and place them on paper overnight. Next morning

there will probably be piles of a fine yellowish powder.
What is this? Pollen dust, you say. Yes. Then
where does it come from? From the pollen cases.
Then these tresses, called catkins, are flower clusters.

But there are no
pistils here. These
flowers, then, are
the stamen flowers.
Where are the pis-
til flowers? Look
above the stamen
flowers for little
urn-shaped bodies,
one or two or three
together. They
stand upright, not
hanging down in
catkins.

FIG. 241. Spray of white-oak leaves and fruit.

The fruit. After the leaves come and the pollen has
been scattered, the stamen flowers, or catkins, fall.
But if everything has gone well with the pistil flower
it begins to grow, because new life has been put into it
by the sperm from the pollen tube joining with the
germ in the embryo case. All through the summer it
grows slowly. It does not ripen so soon as the pea
pod. In the autumn there are the acorns, seated
snugly in their little cups. This is the fruit. The

acorn ripens and falls ; but the tree does not die.
Its life goes on for years, and it bears many other
crops of acorns.

We love the oak. We think of it as a strong and
sturdy tree. We like to play with the acorns and
cups, and sometimes to eat the
meat inside, especially that of
the white oak, after the acorn
has been roast-
ed in the hot
ashes of a fire.
We like to rest
under the shade
of its branches
and to climb to
its top when
the branches
are near the
ground.

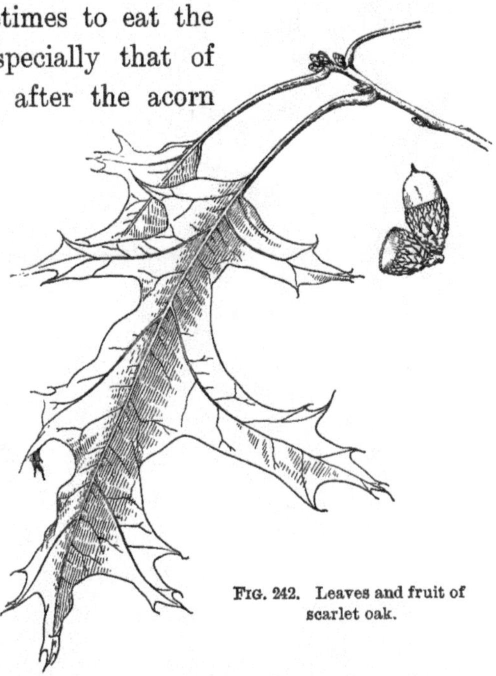

The white
oak forms its
acorns in one

FIG. 242. Leaves and fruit of
scarlet oak.

season. The red oak and the scarlet oak take two
seasons to form their acorns. Can you tell the red
and the scarlet oaks apart by the shape of their leaves ?
Can you tell the white oak from both the red and the
scarlet oaks by the shape of the leaves and the

character of the bark ?   If you were given three acorns in their cups, one of the red oak, one of the scarlet oak, and one of the white oak, could you tell them apart and then name them ?   Do  you know the acorn of the " moss-cup," or " over- cup,"oak? Why is it called by these names? (See Fig. 246.)

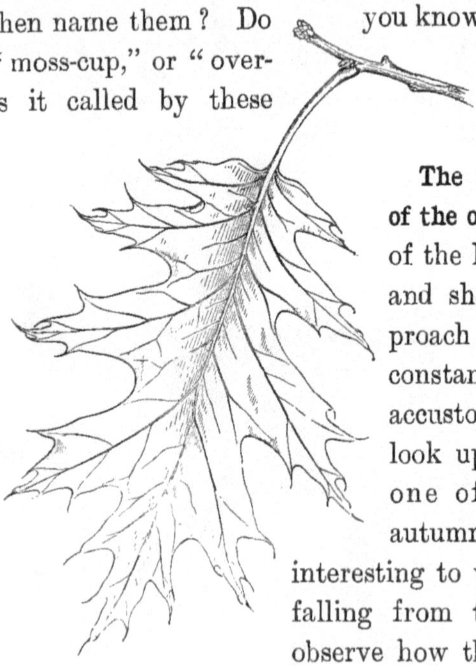

The winter condition of the oak. The falling of the leaves from trees and shrubs on the approach of winter is a constant habit. We are accustomed, perhaps, to look upon it merely as one of the signs of autumn. It is always interesting to watch the leaves falling from the tree and to observe how the movement of the air aids in freeing them

Fig. 243. Leaf of red oak.

from the limb. A gust of wind knocks off troops of them, and sends them scurrying over the field or rolls them in great drifts.

Did you ever think what this shedding of the leaves in the autumn means to the leaf and to the tree ? It is the death of the leaf. But we know that the tree is not dead, for with the on-coming of spring new leaves

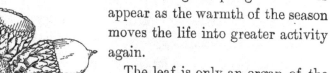
appear as the warmth of the season
moves the life into greater activity
again.

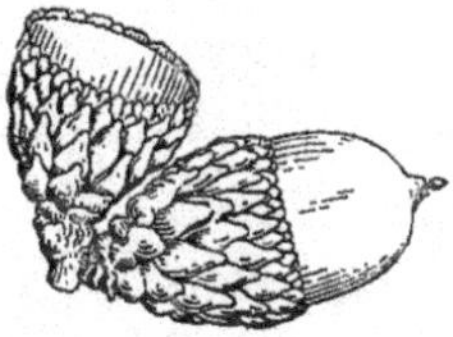

FIG. 244. Fruit of scarlet oak.

The leaf is only an organ of the
tree for summer work, to make
starch food, to dispose of the great
currents of water that are taken up
by the roots, and to do other work
in the preparation of foods and in
getting rid of waste matter. When
the leaf is cast in the
autumn, the tree is only
dropping a member for
which it has no use during

FIG. 245. Fruit of red oak.

the period of winter rest. Some
one may ask why the tree does not
keep its leaves during the winter
and save the growing of new ones
in the spring. It would be fatal
to most of the broad-leaved trees
to keep their green leaves through
the winter. We know that the
leaves give off quantities of water

FIG. 246. Fruit of over-cup oak
or moss-covered oak.

from the tree. During the winter, while the ground
is frozen or cold, the roots can take up very little
water, not nearly so much as the leaves can give off.

The tree has thus acquired a remarkably good habit in laying aside its leaves during the winter, when they

FIG. 247. " Needle " leaves and stamen flowers of pitch pine.

would be of little service, and would even endanger its life if they were retained.

Some trees keep their green leaves through the winter. The pines, spruces, cedars, and other evergreens do. Why is it not danger-ous for them to do so? The leaves of the pines, spruces, and cedars are small and needle-like, or awl shaped, with a thick, hard covering, so that these trees do not lose water so rapidly as the broad-leaved trees do. Then, too, a change takes place in the condition and work of the leaves of such evergreens, so that they lose less water in the winter than during the

FIG. 248. Leaves of American yew, evergreen.

summer. Some of the broad-leaved trees and shrubs are also evergreen and retain their leaves during the winter.

Like the pines and spruces, they cast a crop of leaves
after it has been on the tree for two or more years, a
new crop being grown each year. The live oak, the
rhododendrons, and the mountain laurel are examples
of broad-leaved evergreen trees and shrubs. These
leaves, though they are broad, are thick and have a
hard covering, so that they do not give off so much
water in the winter as thinner and softer leaves
would.

CHAPTER XXVII

LIFE STORY OF FERNS

The fern plant. There are no plants which mean more to us in our home life than ferns. There are no plants which are more generally loved. The refining influence of their presence is constantly felt. Their graceful forms, the beautiful shapes of their leaves, and the restful green of their abundant foliage interest us and satisfy us whenever we see them. If we could only get the maidenhair to grow in our yards as abundantly and easily as the dandelion does, how charming it would be! Many of us would willingly part with some of the dandelions if we could have the maidenhair or Christmas fern in their place.

As we found on page 63 (see Fig. 93), the stems of most of our native ferns are either very short, as in the shield fern, or they are underground stems, as in the bracken fern or sensitive fern. In the polypod, at the north, the stem runs under the leaves or grass, while one in the south runs on the surface of rocks. The climbing fern is found in some parts of New York state, but it is rare. Tree ferns with tall trunks, and other tropical ferns which grow high up on forest trees, may be seen in some large greenhouses.

Fruit dots, spore cases, and spores of ferns. If you take a polypod fern or a Christmas fern (some of the " shield " ferns in the greenhouse will do) and look on the underside of the leaves, you will perhaps see them

FIG. 249. Bank of ferns (after Macmillan).

covered with little dark brown spots. Some people take these for bugs, and scrape them off the fern leaf, for fear they will hurt the fern ! But you can teach them better than that.

Pick a leaf which has these on it, when the brown dots look shiny. Place it on a piece of white paper in a dry room. In a few minutes or an hour you may perhaps see a sprinkling of tiny dust-like bodies on the white paper. You can brush them off with your hand. What are they? They are what we call *spores*. There

FIG. 250. Christmas fern.

is a hard brown wall, and inside a bit of living fern substance. These spores come out of a great many spore cases which are packed together in the fruit dots. So these dark bodies on the underside of the leaf, instead of being bugs which are harmful to plants, are fruit dots with spore cases and spores in them.

If the fern plant is making so many of these tiny spores, each containing a little bit of living fern substance, we would better not scrape them off, for they must be for some good purpose in the life of the fern. If you examine a bracken fern, maidenhair fern, and some other kinds, you will find that the fruit dots are of different shapes, and that some of them are under a flap at the edge of the leaf.

Does the fern plant have flowers? The fern plant does not have flowers as the flowering plants do. Nor

does the fern plant have seeds. It will be interesting
to know, then, how new fern plants are formed.

How new fern plants are formed. We have already

FIG. 251. Little spleenwort fern.

learned that most ferns bear " fruit dots " or lines on
the underside of certain leaves. We also know that
many tiny spores are in the rounded spore cases which
are packed together to form the fruit dots. When

these spores are ripe and have been scattered, some of them fall in damp places on the ground, or on a rotting

log in the woods. Here this tiny bit of living fern substance begins to grow, and the living matter inside the hard brown coat pushes its way out through a split in the wall; in a few weeks it has grown into a tiny heart-shaped bit of plant tissue no bigger round than a radish seed, or a small pea, and as thin and delicate as fine tissue paper. This little object, shown in Fig. 254, is a *fern*

FIG. 252. "Fruit" dots of the common polypody fern.

prothallium (*pro-thal'li-um*). On the underside are numbers of rootlets, like root hairs, and two kinds of tiny pockets. This little prothallium now gives birth to the embryo fern plant.

How the embryo of the fern plant starts. The germ cell is in one of the large pockets near the deep notch in the prothallium, and the sperms are in the round pockets. One of the sperms swims into

FIG. 253. "Fruit" dots of the maidenhair fern.

the germ pocket, unites with the germ, and then the germ grows into the embryo fern plant.

The fern prothallium and embryo compared to a seed.
The fern prothallium, with the young embryo fern

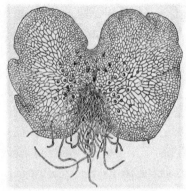

attached, might be compared to a seed of one of the higher plants, where the embryo is surrounded by a food tissue known as the endosperm, as in the corn. *This endosperm is in fact a prothallium of the higher plant.* In the corn seed it is shown as in Fig. 44. Some of it is still left inside

FIG. 254. Prothallium of fern, bearing the germ and sperm pockets. This is a view from the underside, and shows the rootlets also.

the embryo case. But in the pea, bean, and acorn it is all used up as food by the embryo and stored in the cotyledons. The only way in which the prothallium with the embryo of the fern differs from the seed of the corn or bean is in the fact that the prothallium is green (with chlorophyll), that it has been shed from the spore case, and has been developed as an independent individual. If the fern prothallium were not green, but were wrapped around the embryo and still in the spore case, it would be a seed. When the

FIG. 255. Embryo fern still attached to the prothallium.

young embryo fern grows large enough to burst out of
the prothallium, when the root strikes into the soil and
the cotyledon or first leaf rises upward, as shown in

Fig. 255, it is doing precisely
the same thing that a seed
does when it germinates,
strikes root, and lifts its leaves
and stem upward to the light.

The generations of the fern.
The life story of the fern
reveals to us *two generations*,
the *prothallium* and the *fern
plant*. They can live independent of each other. Each
one can take water and food
from the soil. With the leaf-
green each one can make its
own starch food. The pro-

FIG. 256. The walking fern, taking
steps down a hillside.

thallium starts from the spore on the fern plant, and
the fern plant starts from the germ in the prothallium.
The two generations therefore alternate with each
other, as it were. In the corn, the bean, and other
plants of this kind there seems to be only one generation. This is because one part of it, the prothallium
generation, is packed away and hidden in the embryo
case as endosperm, while the other part is hidden in
the pollen and pollen tube. Most plants, then, have

two generations in their lives. It is only in the ferns, however, and their near relatives that the two genera-

FIG. 257. The bracken fern in company with the "sturdy" oak (after Macmillan).

tions can exist independently. In the flowering plants the prothallium generation is dependent, and hidden away in the embryo case.

CHAPTER XXVIII

THE LIFE STORY OF THE MOSS

Mossy banks and trees. Those who live near the woods, or who have a chance to go to the woods or mountains in summer, delight in finding a carpet of moss on the ground or on some shady bank. The slender, short stems covered with delicate leaves make a velvety cushion of green. We know that these tiny plants love the cool shade, for, except in the cold arctic or alpine regions, we find them growing freely only in or near the woods. The tree trunks, too, in moist, cool, shady places are often covered with moss. There are sometimes tiny tufts and mats on the ground in open fields, by roadsides and streets, even in cities, and in the cracks of old stone walls. But the mosses do not attract us much in these places because they are so scattered and small.

FIG. 258. Moss-covered trunk.

The pigeon-wheat moss. Who knows the pigeon-wheat moss? Well, here is a picture of a clump of it. In the open wood, or near the woods on damp ground, you may see it in clumps or in large patches.

The moss is more interesting to study when it is in fruit, because then one can read more of its life story.

FIG. 259. Clump of "pigeon-wheat" moss.

The moss in Fig. 259 is in fruit. There are little stalks that rise out from the ends of the leafy stem with a little capsule on the end of each stalk. Sometimes this capsule is covered with a large, pointed, woolly hood, and perhaps the appearance of numbers of these suggested tiny wheat stalks and heads. Lift the hood off. There is the capsule with a little lid on the end. You can remove this lid with a pin. There is the mouth of the capsule with a fringe of tiny teeth that you can just see with your sharp eyes. If you thrust the pin into the capsule, you will bring out a dusty powder, like pollen, or like fern spores. These are moss spores; the moss capsule, then, is the spore case.

You should understand that the beautiful red, brown, and green plants so common along the ocean shore, and called popularly " sea mosses," are not true mosses. They are *algæ*. The pond scums are algæ also. Then the " hanging moss," or Florida moss, which is so common in the Southern States, is not a true moss. It is a flowering plant. It bears true flowers and also forms seeds. The true mosses do not have flowers, nor do they form true seeds. The spores of the moss form a green thread-like growth on the soil or rotten wood, which resembles some of the " pond scums." From this thread-like growth the leafy moss stem arises.

FIG. 260. Branched plant of "pigeon-wheat" moss, showing "hood" on spore case at left.

CHAPTER XXIX

LIFE STORY OF MUSHROOMS

Mushrooms, too, have a story to tell. They live out of sight most of the time. When they show themselves they do so only for a short time. They seem to come up in a single night, and many of them do. But

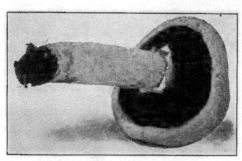

others may be several days in coming up.

They keep hidden most of the time in the form of cords, or strings, until they have spread themselves out in

FIG. 261. The common mushroom showing stem, cap, ring, gills.

reach of a great feast of food in the ground or in wood. Then the mushroom part can grow very fast, and spring out from its hiding place into the light.

So if you wish to read the story of mushrooms you must be quick about it, for they do not stay long. The common mushroom, like many others, is shaped like an umbrella; it has a handle, a ring, rays on the underside, and a cover. The handle is the *stem*, the ring is called a *ring* or *collar*, the rays are called the *gills*

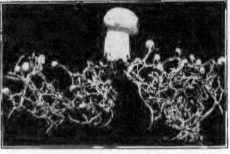

FIG. 262. A spore print of the common mushroom.

of the mushroom, and the cover is the *cap*.

The spores. Cut off the stem of the common mushroom, a specimen just expanded. Lay the cap, gills down, on white paper for several hours or overnight. The paper underneath the cap becomes covered with a very fine dark brown powder. These are *spores*, not seeds, for the mushroom has no seeds. The spores take the place of seed. They can start new points of growth for the mushroom.

FIG. 263. Spawn and young buttons of the mushroom.

Spawn of mushrooms. Where the common mushroom is growing in the field, dig some up with a trowel and search in the soil for delicate white cords. If a

bed where mushrooms are grown is near, you will
find more of these white cords in the soil.   This the
gardeners call
spawn.   We call
it *mycelium.*
Gardeners take
this spawn and
sow it in new
beds.   It spreads
and increases,
and makes more
mushrooms, after
it has feasted on

FIG. 264.   Buttons of the common mushroom just
coming through the sod.

the food in the bed.   So in the field
or woods this spawn spreads through
the earth.   It takes up water and
food from the soil as roots do, and
yet the spawn is not a root.

The beginning of the mushroom.
If you can get a quantity of this
spawn of the common mushroom,
wash out the soil.   Look on the cords
for very small round bodies.   You
will find some very small, perhaps
no larger than a mustard seed.   You
may find others as large as a marble.

FIG. 265. A deadly poisonous mushroom with a
"bag" over the base of
the stem. (Deadly ama-
nita.)

These are the buttons, the beginning of the mushroom.

In the ones as large as marbles the upper end is enlarged.
This is the beginning of the cap. When it reaches this

size the mush-
room grows very
fast. But the
spawn may grow
several months,
or a year, feeding
on decaying plant
material in the
ground before
any mushrooms
appear.

FIG. 236. A toadstool good to eat, with a "bag" on the
base of the stem. (Royal agaric.)

The common
mushroom, which
grows in the fields
and is cultivated
in mushroom
houses, has pink
gills when young,
and dark brown
gills when old. It
has a white or
brownish cap, a
stem and a ring.

FIG. 267. A poisonous mushroom, or toadstool, whichever
you choose to call it, with no true "bag" on the stem,
only scales which represent one. (The fly amanita.)

Other mushrooms. There are many kinds of mushrooms; many are good to eat, and some are very

poisonous.　No one should gather mushrooms to eat unless he knows very well the kind he picks.　Some of the poisonous ones have a cup or bag around the lower end of the stem.　But some which have this bag or cup are good to eat.　So you would bet-ter read their stories, and not pick them for eating until you know the kinds as well as you know the faces of your playmates.

FIG. 268.　The ink cap.

If you should pick a basket full of different kinds in the woods, and place the caps down on white paper, you would catch the spores. You would probably find that the spores in some cases are black, in others brown, yellow, rose-colored, or white.

The ink mushrooms. These are curious and interesting.　Soon after

FIG. 269.　The ink cap turning to ink.

they come up, the gills and much of the cap turn to a black, inky fluid which you could write with. One kind is called "ink cap," another is called the "shaggy mane," or "horse-tail." These are good to eat before they turn to ink.

FIG. 270. The shaggy mane, or horse-tail mushroom. Also an ink mushroom.

Puffballs and earth stars. Did you ever see puffballs, and pinch one to see the cloud of dust which flies out? Some people call them "devil's snuff-box." They grow from spawn in the ground and in rotten wood too. The cloud of dust is full of spores, which start more spawn to make more puffballs, and so the life story keeps spinning round and round. You have heard of the starfish; did you ever hear of the star fungus or star mushroom? We call it earth star, a pretty name, because it is shaped like a star and grows on the ground. It is a near relative of the puffball.

Some will tell you that such interesting plants as the ferns, mosses, mushrooms, and puffballs are *cryptogams*, and that therefore you should not try to

FIG. 271. The puffball, or devil's snuffbox.

read the stories they have to tell.   But why call them
cryptogams?   That is a terrible word that ought to be
blotted out of the English language.   Why not call

Fig. 272.   The earth star.

them plants, as they are ?   They are just as much God's
creatures as the dandelion and thistle and smartweed
are.   They are just as interesting, too, and mean as
much in our lives as they do.

PART V

BATTLES OF PLANTS IN THE WORLD

CHAPTER XXX

THE STRUGGLES OF A WHITE PINE

Many seeds but few trees. If all the seeds of the
white pine which fall year after year from the trees in
the forest and from individual trees in the fields should
grow and form trees, the world could not contain them.
For every seed ripened the chances of becoming a tree
are very few. It seems a great waste of energy on the
part of the tree to form so many seeds when so few can
ever hope to become trees. But it is a very fortunate
provision of Nature that a single plant should ripen so
many seeds where we know the chances for life are so
small. Many trees bear thousands and thousands of
seeds, but where are the young pines? Often there
are none to be seen in the neighborhood of very prolific trees.

The struggle for a start. From some of the trees
the seeds fall on cultivated ground, and if the seedlings

start they are plowed under while the crops are being tended. Others may fall on the hard meadow or grass land. The seed can-not bury itself here. If it germinates, the root cannot go deep enough to furnish water and food. In the forest many seeds fall on the thick carpet of dry leaves

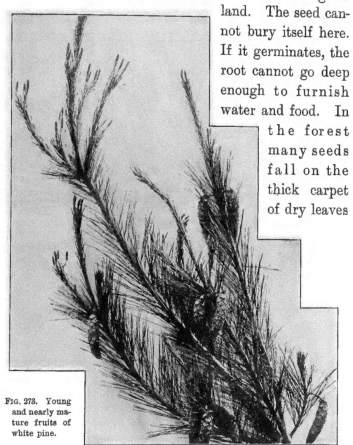

FIG. 273. Young and nearly ma-ture fruits of white pine.

and are unable to reach the soft, moist humus, or earth below. All these seeds perish. But sometimes

a cultivated field may be abandoned for several years
and left to grow up to weeds, grass, and bushes. Animals sometimes disturb the leaves in the forest and

FIG. 274. Stamen flowers of the white pine.

root up the fresh soil. The woodsman may tear open
other places when he drags his logs along the ground.
Large trees uprooted by the wind expose an area of

moist soil.   Seeds which fall in these places have a
better chance for life.   Some of them become covered

in the soil by the beating rains.   They
are covered at unequal depths.   The
struggle for a start begins.   The good
seed which is covered by the soil and
moistened by the rains germinates.
Before all the roots are fixed deep
enough in the soil the sun comes out
and several days, perhaps weeks, go
by without rain.   The surface soil
dries.   The seedlings which were
lightly covered perish.   The few

FIG. 275.   At left winged
seed of white pine,
at right a scale with
two pine seeds still in
position.

which have a good hold in the soil by
being buried deeper than the others
have plenty of water and food.   The
crown of leaves is lifted above the soil,
and the embryo case is cast off.   The
seedling has pushed its stem and leaves
up to the light, and its roots are spreading in the soil to secure it more firmly.
There are others around it almost within
touch.   Troops of these more fortunate
creatures are scattered here and there.

FIG. 276.   Seedling of
white pine just com-
ing up.

The struggle with other vegetation.
Now begins a competition among the seedlings and
other plants for mastery of the position.   Weeds, grasses,

vines, perhaps young shrubs and oaks, spring up, for the soil is thick with the seeds of other plants as prolific in seed-bearing as the pine. Many of these grow faster now than the pine seedlings. The weeds and grass soon tower above them and hide them. It looks as if the pine seedlings would be choked out. But they can do fairly well in the shade; better, perhaps, than the weeds think, if they are capable of doing such a thing. The pine seedlings do not hurry. They bide their time. They are making long and useful roots. They are preparing for a long struggle for life.

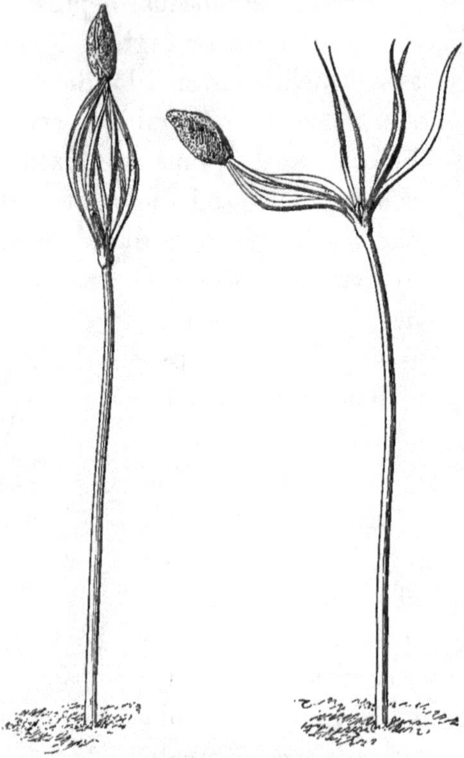

FIG. 277. White-pine seedlings casting seed coats or embryo cases.

The score after the first season. In the autumn let us take count of the contest. The weeds **raced swiftly**

and got far ahead.   But they have exhausted themselves.   They have ripened many seeds, but they die;
their leaves wither and dry up.   This lets in more light
for the tiny pine seedlings.   The autumn winds and
rain beat on the dead weeds and break many of them
down.   The snow finishes many more.   In the spring,

FIG. 278.   Evergreens and broad-leaved trees just getting above the
weeds and grass (Alabama).

when the snow disappears, it looks as if the little seedlings had another chance.   If the winter was cold and
the ground bare for a part of the time, perhaps some
were frozen to death.   The second and third seasons
come and go.   The weeds flourish each year just as
before.   They hide the tiny pines, but they cannot
choke them out.   The little trees grow slowly but
surely.

Another enemy than weeds to struggle against. Perhaps, in the first season, or the second, or the third,

FIG. 279. Young white pines getting a start. Three ages of pine trees are shown (New York).

or even later, another foe appears which pursues different tactics from those of the weeds. It is a tiny

fungus, or mold, of delicate gossamer-like threads.   It
is apt to make its attack on the seedlings in wet
weather, just at the surface of the ground.   The
threads of the mold make little holes in the stem and
grow inside.   They feed on the stem, dissolving so

FIG. 280. Young " bull pines " getting a start (Colorado).

much of it that it shrinks away and becomes thin and
soft, and dead at the ground level.   The little pine
cannot hold itself up.   It topples over to the ground
and dies.   We say it "damps off," because it appears
to rot and die on account of the wet ground.   But it
was the little plant mold that killed it.   Though the

mold was very much smaller than the pine, it made a

FIG. 281. Four giant white pines
(New York).

successful attack. Many of the seedlings may fall from the attacks of this insidious foe.

The pines get larger. Each year those that remain get higher. They seem to make up in size what they have lost in number. They grow at a more rapid rate now and are beginning to outstrip and shade the weeds. The weeds and grass cannot endure the shade as well as the little pines could.

As the pines get higher the branches reach out and nearly cut off the light from the ground. Finally the weeds and grass can no longer grow underneath them. The few pines remaining have overcome the weeds.

Other competitors appear.   There were, perhaps, some
acorns, or beechnuts, or the seeds of other trees in the
ground.   A few of these got a start.   Some may have
started before the pines did.   The pines have grown

FIG. 282.   Conifers overtopping broad-leaved trees in the forest (New Hampshire).

out of the way of the weeds now.   In fact, they never
feared the weeds.   They were grateful for the shade,
perhaps, while they were young.   Now the young
oaks and beeches, elms, etc., are more sturdy and

dangerous competitors. They do not die at the end
of the season. They grow larger and larger. During

the summer their broad leaves make
a great deal more shade than the
pine leaves do. Some of the pines get
covered and crowded as time goes on.
Some of the smaller ones die. This
struggle is renewed year after year.
One foot, eighteen inches, or two feet,
the trees add to their height annually.
Their limbs reach out and interlock as
if in actual physical struggle. The
dense foliage on the upper branches
cuts off much light below. The lower

FIG. 283. An enemy of
pines, a shelving
"mushroom," grow-
ing from a spruce
hemlock.

branches
die away.
The tall,
smooth trunks of forest
trees appear below the rising tops, which get higher
and higher. The smaller
trees die and fall to the
ground. It is a struggle
now between the taller
and finer pines and the
taller and sturdier oaks.

FIG. 284. Spawn of the "mushroom" shown
in Fig. 283 as it makes its way through the
wood of the tree.

It is a battle of giants, a
contest for the "survival of the fittest." Here and

there between the round tops of the oak are clear views of the sky above. Through these openings the straight shaft, or "leader," of the pine shoots upward in its more rapid growth. Soon the pines begin here and there to tower above the other trees. Their branches reach out and elbow their way above the tops of the oaks. The pines have risen above the other trees of the forest and

FIG. 285. Effects of fire in forest (New Jersey).

hold almost undisputed sway. It now becomes a struggle of pine with pine to see which is the stronger.

Enemies of old pines. As the conquered trees have fallen they have crushed down others, or they have broken large limbs and bruised the trunks. The wood and timber enemies, in the shape of the mushroom and bracket fungi, enter the wound by tiny threads and rot the "heart" of the tree, so that it is weakened and hollow. Fires run through the forest, flashing through the leaves and burning longer in the dead logs. Sound trunks are scorched and sometimes killed, which makes other entrance places for their enemies. Insects, in the shape of " borers " and " saw-flies," wound and destroy.

Man sometimes a great enemy of the forest. Then the woodman may come to level the giants with axe and saw. Against him the pines have no means of

defense. The finest trees are cut. Here is one which has suffered from a fungus enemy, and so has a hollow trunk. The woodman spares that tree because it is of no value to him. It is left standing alone to tell the tale of the proud pine forest and its grand struggle for mastery.

Then man begins his " civilizing influences." The old fallen trunks

FIG. 286. A bracket " mushroom " growing from a maple.

and the brushwood are burned. The stumps are gradually rooted out. The ground is plowed and planted. Here and there are a few of the remaining giants which man for one reason or another leaves in his cultivated field. One of these is the towering hollow trunk of the pine. It has the look of centuries. It has ceased to advance. Near the top of the tall trunk are great branches. Buildings spring up where once its comrades stood. Many people come to admire this battle-scarred

FIG. 287. Giants of the forest felled by man.

pine. Some one puts a seat near it, and tired travelers rest under this grand old pine. A vine is planted, which climbs up on the great bare trunk and gives it a bit of coloring in summer.

The result of a tussle with a gale. One cold winter day, when the ground was white with the deep snow, a wind came out of the northwest which grew to a gale. A terrific contest came on between the wind and the old pine. Younger elms and oaks, spruces and pines, grown up since the pine's old comrades had disappeared, bent their limbs and trunks with the gale and

FIG. 288. White pine. Result of a tussle with a gale.

rocked to and fro. Now it seemed as if the slender limbs would be torn off. But they were lithe and yielding, and recovered and straightened from each heavy thrust of the gale. The old pine stood proud and fixed, its litheness of limb nearly gone. A fierce gust of the wind snapped off a huge limb like a pipe-stem and dashed it down into the snow bank. Firmly and stiffly did the old pine hold out against each onslaught of the gale, but fiercer came the gusts and half a dozen limbs lay half buried in the snow, and only the stout stubs stood out where once large branches were. Finally the wind subsided, and the old pine still stands, with only its topmost branches left. It is sad to think that the time is near at hand when the old tree must go down.

CHAPTER XXXI

STRUGGLES AGAINST WIND

WHILE the wind is of very great help to many plants in scattering their seed, and thus giving rise to new and young individuals, it is often an enemy against which plants have to contend. Hurricanes and cyclones sometimes sweep down large tracts of forest trees. In some localities there are prevailing winds from one direction. These winds are so frequent and of such force that the tree cannot maintain its normal erect and symmetrical growth. Such prevailing winds often occur along the seacoast or near large lakes, and in mountainous regions, where there are certain well-established and marked differences in temperature and air pressures which tend to create continuous currents in definite directions.

In some places along the seacoast and on mountain heights, especially on the sides of mountains or on elevations in mountain passes, the strong winds are nearly all from one direction and of such force that the entire tree leans with the wind; or the trunk may grow erect while all the branches are on the leeward side. The young lithe branches which come out on

FIG. 289. Effects of wind on forest (New Hampshire).

the windward side are bent around in the opposite
direction. The wind keeps them bent in this direction
so continuously that the growth and hardening of the
wood finally fixes the branch in that position, — a good
example of the force of habit. The young branch finds

Fig. 290. Tree permanently bent by wind (coast of New Jersey).

it easier to bend with the wind than to resist it. When
it becomes old this habit is fixed, and the bent and
gnarled branches could not straighten even if the wind
should moderate. Very interesting examples are seen
in regions where the trade winds occur. The trade

FIG. 291. Old cypress trees, permanently bent by wind
(Monterey, coast of California).

FIG. 292. Main trunk straight, branches all bent and fixed to one side by
wind from one direction (Rocky Mountains).

winds are not very strong, but they blow constantly in one direction. Fig. 293 represents a silk-cotton tree on the island of Nassau, in the Atlantic Ocean. The tree is inclined as a result of the constant wind. Where this tree is exposed to the wind, buttresses (bracing roots) are developed at the base of the trunk. It is said that the silk-cotton tree when growing in the

Fig. 293.   Tree permanently bent by trade wind (Nassau).

forest, where the wind does not exercise such force on it, has no buttresses. The one-sided development of the banyan tree (Fig. 295), influenced by the trade winds, is interesting to compare with the one shown in Fig. 294, where, in the absence of a constant wind in one direction, a symmetrical development has taken place.

FIG. 294. Banyan tree spreading equally on all sides from a central trunk where the tree started, and taking root as it spreads to give support (photograph, Rau, No. 6109).

FIG. 295. Banyan tree moved in one direction by trade wind. The older portion of the tree is at the right.

CHAPTER XXXII

STRUGGLES FOR TERRITORY

The struggle is going on around us all the time. There are opportunities for all of us to see some of

FIG. 296. Sycamores, grasses, and weeds, having a hard time starting on a rock bed.

these struggles among the plants themselves, and the struggles of plants with the condition of the soil or weather or other surroundings. Go into woods or

244

fields almost any day and you will see some sign of the warfare going on. A grapevine has covered over several small trees and is smothering and weighing them down. The grass has stopped growing under trees which branch and produce dense foliage near the ground. When the water is drained from a marshy

FIG. 297. Island with perpendicular sides in Lake Massawiepie, Adirondacks.

piece of ground, plants from the drier ground rush in, and soon the character of the vegetation is changed. Did you ever observe how much quicker the grass or cultivated plants wither in dry weather near large trees? The tree takes water from the soil. It cuts off the water supply of other plants. It takes their food also. There is often a struggle among the branches of a tree to see which one shall get most of the light and thus outlive its competitors.

Certain soils are congenial to certain plants. If all plants could grow in all situations, we should have fewer kinds of plants because there would be so many competitors for every foot of ground. But some plants have found one kind of soil congenial to them, and other plants prefer another kind of soil. So, many plants leave certain territory undisputed, and only enter into a contest if some favorable changes take place in those localities, provided, of course, their seeds get in there. We do sometimes find a few plants struggling in a very uncongenial soil, but they never

FIG. 298.   Island in Raquette River, Adirondacks, with sloping sides and providing different kinds of territory.

become real competitors with the plants which like to grow there. They are struggling only with the physical forces of nature, not with other plants.

Struggles of plants on border territory. The different territories which are congenial to different plants border on one another. Sometimes the border is very abrupt, so that there is no struggle on the part of the plants in one territory to cross over into the other. But in a great many cases the change from one territory to another is gradual. In these

FIG. 299. Border of lake with sloping shore. Cocklebur on the right fighting with grasses on the left (Ithaca, N.Y.).

cases the border line becomes the seat of a fierce struggle for occupation between the plants of the two adjoining areas.

These struggles are very commonly seen along the borders of lakes, ponds, or streams, where the ground slopes gradually down to the water edge and out into deep water. So, also, on the borders of marshes or where there is a gradual difference in elevation from a moist soil up to one which is drier. Here we often see various kinds of plants drawn up in battle array defending and holding their ground.   The arrow-leaf likes to grow in soil covered with water on the borders of lakes and ponds, where the water is not too deep. The cat-tail flag prefers a little less depth of water, and it contends for the ground nearer the shore, where the

FIG. 300.   Plants drawn in battle array on shore line of lake (Ithaca, N.Y.).

water is very shallow.   The Joe-Pye weed and boneset like very moist soil near the water.

In this picture (Fig. 300) you see such a contest going on, and the lines of battle sharply drawn.   Near this place you could see an army of rushes occupying the same kind of territory that the arrow-leaf occupies here, because the same conditions were congenial to it and the rush drove the arrow-leaf out.   So, on such dis-puted grounds, struggles for possession go on between the kinds of plants which like that territory, and the weaker ones are often crowded out of existence.

CHAPTER XXXIII

PLANT SOCIETIES

Plant associations. Plants which have congenial dispositions often grow together in harmony on the same territory. There is room for several different kinds, just as there is room for many small stones in the spaces between large stones in a pile. Moreover,

FIG. 301. Peat-bog formation with heaths, cranberries, sedges, etc., growing on it, and all advancing to fill in the pond. This is a plant " atoll."

several kinds of plants of the same size may have · congenial dispositions toward each other, so that they can live peaceably together. No one of these kinds tries to cover all the ground. They are content with a spot here and there. At least they have not very pugnacious dispositions, nor are they so forward as to crowd themselves in and push out the others. Plants which live together peaceably in this way form societies. They are really social in their dispositions, and often several kinds in one society are dependent on the others. They could not live alone. They need something to cling to, or they need protection from the great light and heat of the sun.

Even where the rushes, and cat-tails, and arrow-leaf, and Joe-Pye weed seem to occupy the ground, there are many other kinds of plants which are not so large that fit in between the tall ones or cling to them, or float in the water.

Peculiar societies of peat bogs. When you visit the peat bogs or sphagnum moors, where the peat moss or sphagnum grows, you will find a society of peculiar plants. These plants like cold water and other singular surroundings for their stems and roots. Their disposition is so unusual in this respect that none of the common plants you are familiar with in the fields and woods would go into their society or live in their territory, unless after many years the character of the territory should change so that it would be more congenial.

Growing along with the peat moss you will often find cranberries, Labrador tea, the curious pitcher plant, and many other plants with thick leaves which are retentive of moisture. The plants that associate with the peat moss must be those which give off water into the air slowly, since the cold water and certain acids about their roots in the dead peat below the surface prevent the roots from taking up water rapidly.

The vegetation on the margin of the peat bog. On the margin of the peat bog, where the ground is drier

FIG. 302. Plants marching into the sea. They have advanced from the trees at the left in about two hundred years.

and contains more soil, you may see the plants drawn up in battle array. The societies are struggling among themselves, and are also pushing their way slowly out into the peat. The story of the advance is plainly told by the size and age of the vegetation, as well as by its difference in character.

Many of the peat bogs were once small ponds or lakes. The peat moss and other plants which find shallow water a congenial place to grow in begin marching out from the edge of the water toward the center of the pond. The stems of the peat die below and grow above. So in this way they build up a floor or platform in the water. The dead peat now in the water below does not thoroughly rot, as the leaves do in the moist ground of the forest, because the water shuts out the air. The partly dead stems of the moss pile up quite fast in making the platform, which sometimes is entirely composed of peat. Other plants may grow along with the peat. Their dead bodies also help to build up this floor beneath.

The army of peat and other water plants continues to march out toward the center of the pond, though slowly. Finally, in many cases the line around the shore meets in the center and the pond is filled up, the floor having been extended entirely across. But they keep on adding each year to the floor, raising it higher and higher, until it is high enough and dry enough for the marching armies of the dry land grasses, shrubs, and trees. At length a forest comes to stand on the floor built across the pond by the peat moss and the other members of its society.

Forest societies. There are many kinds of forest societies, just as there are of herbaceous plants. These depend on the elevation, the action of the climate, soil, etc., as well as on the kinds of trees. Forests in the arctic regions are different from those of the temperate

Fig. 303. Vegetation on border of marsh.

zones, and these are different from the forests of the tropics. The society may be at first mixed, cone-bearing, and evergreen trees, with broad-leaved trees. In the end of the struggle some of these are likely to be crowded out. Where the forest growth is even and the leafy tops cut off much of the light, the forest floor

FIG. 304. Coniferous forest society, white pine.

will be covered with leaves ; there will be an absence of shrubs and herbs, except the shade-loving ones, and the wood will be open below and free from " undergrowth."

When the forest is open above because of the unequal growth of the trees, or because of the destruction of

FIG. 305. Edge of broad-leaved forest society in winter.

some of the larger trees, light will enter and encourage a greater or less development of undergrowth,— young trees, shrubs, flowers, grass, etc. Then, too, you observe in the forests the great numbers of mushrooms, singular but beautiful and important members of a forest society. Some of them, however, become enemies of trees, entering at wounds and rotting out the heart. Others attack the leaves, and by injuring or destroying these food-getting organs weaken the life of the tree. Others attack branches and deform or blight them.

Mosses and lichens, in the temperate and arctic forests, greatly influence the character of the tree trunk which they cover and color. Those hanging on branches give a grotesque appearance and sometimes do injury. In sub-tropical and tropical forests there is a tendency to a change of position of the smaller members of the society from the forest floor to the tree tops, where hanging moss and tree-dwelling orchids and ferns abound.

Desert societies. The oddest looking of plant societies are desert societies, — the great trunks of different kinds of cactus, with no leaves on them, or the sprawling *opuntias*, many of the cacti covered with spines. These large fleshy trunks do not lose water so rapidly as thin leaves do; so these plants are well suited to grow in the dry climate of the desert, where the soil is often parched and little water can be found by the plants. This character of the vegetation is the result of ages of warfare with uncongenial conditions. All plants not suited to grow here either have been

Fig. 306. Desert society chiefly cactus (Arizona).

driven out or have not been able to enter. Those which could take on these forms of the cacti, or of the yuccas, etc., bore trunks with a few hard-skinned leaves at the tops, survived, and now find these conditions quite congenial to them.

Fence-corner and roadside societies. Not every one of you can go to the desert to see the desert societies,

FIG. 307.   Desert society, chiefly yucca.

or to see the arctic or tropical societies. You must be content with pictures of them. But nearly every one can see plant societies near at hand that are interesting if looked at in the right way. Some of you, in large cities, perhaps do not often see fence

FIG. 308. A roadside society in low ground. Jewel weed attacked by dodder.

corners (though there are some in the heart of New York city) or country roads. But you surely get an outing into the country once in a while. If you don't, you ought to, that's all. Then you can study fence-corner societies, roadside societies, field and forest societies, the brambles, weeds, berries, golden-rod, and asters, and the new-mown hay.

Garden societies. Most of you can have, at least, a garden society; a little plot of ground where you can plant seeds or see the flowers grow, and in the corner of the garden a place where the wild flowers and weeds may struggle.

Plant societies in windows. Here, I am sure, all can have a plant society for observation. Fasten on a window ledge a long box, with broken bits of crockery in the bottom and garden soil on top. There should be an outlet in one end to drain off the surplus water. Here you can grow peas, beans, and other plants to see them struggle with each other and turn toward the light. In another box, or in pots, you can raise some flowers, — geraniums, primroses, and other suitable ones.

You can also have a water-plant society by fitting up an aquarium in a well-lighted window. This can be made by using a large glass vessel, or perhaps some small ones can be made by using fruit jars or broad pans. Put some garden soil in the bottom to supply some of the food. Then nearly fill the vessel with water. In these aquaria you can place *elodea*, the pond scum, and other water plants; but do not have them too crowded. With several of these aquaria and the window gardens you will have an opportunity of learning some interesting habits of plants.

While you can learn many interesting things about plants from window-garden societies, you should not be content with these mere glimpses of the habits and social life of plants. The best place to study plants is in their own homes; so improve every opportunity to visit the fields and woods, become acquainted with some of the flowers and trees, and especially to study their behavior under different conditions and at different seasons of the year. When the fields and woods cannot be visited, the parks and gardens will furnish many subjects from which you can read most interesting stories if you will only try to interpret the sign language by means of which the trees and flowers express to us their lives and work.

INDEX

263

264　　　　　　　　INDEX

ADVERTISEMENTS.

NATURE STUDY

ATKINSON'S FIRST STUDIES OF PLANT LIFE.
By GEORGE FRANCIS ATKINSON of Cornell University. For introduction,
60 cents.

THE JANE ANDREWS BOOKS.
The Seven Little Sisters. With new full-page illustrations. For introduction,
50 cents.
Each and All. With new full-page illustrations. For introduction, 50 cents.
Stories Mother Nature Told her Children. With new full-page illustrations.
For introduction, 50 cents.
My Four Friends. For introduction, 40 cents.

STICKNEY'S STUDY AND STORY NATURE READERS.
By J. H. STICKNEY, author of the Stickney Readers.
Earth and Sky. For introduction, 30 cents.
Pets and Companions. For introduction, 30 cents.
Bird World. By J. H. STICKNEY, assisted by RALPH HOFFMANN. For intro-
duction, 60 cents.

STRONG'S ALL THE YEAR ROUND.
By FRANCES L. STRONG of the Teachers' Training School, St. Paul, Minn.
Part I., Autumn. Part II., Winter. Part III., Spring. Each, for intro
duction, 30 cents.

EDDY'S FRIENDS AND HELPERS.
Compiled by SARAH J. EDDY. For introduction, 60 cents.

GOULD'S MOTHER NATURE'S CHILDREN.
By ALLEN WALTON GOULD. For introduction, 60 cents.

LANE'S ORIOLE STORIES.
By M. A. L. LANE. For introduction, 28 cents.

LONG'S WAYS OF WOOD FOLK. (First Series.)
By WILLIAM J. LONG. For introduction, 50 cents.

LONG'S WILDERNESS WAYS. (Second Series.)
By WILLIAM J. LONG. For introduction, 45 cents.

MORLEY'S LITTLE WANDERERS.
By MARGARET WARNER MORLEY. For introduction, 30 cents.

WEED'S STORIES OF INSECT LIFE. (First Series.)
By CLARENCE M. WEED, Professor of Zoölogy and Entomology in the New
Hampshire College of Agriculture and the Mechanic Arts. For introduction,
25 cents.

MURTFELDT AND WEED'S STORIES OF INSECT LIFE. (Second Series.)
By MARY E. MURTFELDT and CLARENCE MOORES WEED. For introduction,
30 cents.

WEED'S SEED-TRAVELLERS.
By CLARENCE M. WEED. For introduction, 25 cents.

BEAL'S SEED DISPERSAL.
By W. J. BEAL, Professor of Botany and Forestry in Michigan State Agricultural
College. For introduction, 35 cents.

BURT'S LITTLE NATURE STUDIES FOR LITTLE PEOPLE.
From the Essays of JOHN BURROUGHS. Edited by MARY E. BURT.
**Volume I. A Primer and a First Reader. Volume II. A Second Reader
and a Third Reader.** Each, for introduction, 25 cents.

BERGEN'S GLIMPSES AT THE PLANT WORLD.
By FANNY D. BERGEN. For introduction, 50 cents.

HALE'S LITTLE FLOWER PEOPLE.
By GERTRUDE ELISABETH HALE. For introduction, 40 cents.

GINN & COMPANY, Publishers,

Boston.   New York.   Chicago.   San Francisco
Atlanta.   Dallas.   Columbus.   London.

THE JANE ANDREWS BOOKS

The Seven Little Sisters Who Live on the Round Ball That Floats in the Air. Cloth. 121 pages. With new full-page illustrations. For introduction, 50 cents.

Each and All; The Seven Little Sisters Prove Their Sisterhood. Cloth. 162 pages. With new full-page illustrations. For introduction, 50 cents.

The Stories Mother Nature Told Her Children. Cloth. 161 pages. With new full-page illustrations. For introduction, 50 cents.

Ten Boys Who Lived on the Road from Long Ago to Now. Cloth. 243 pages. With new full-page illustrations. For introduction, 50 cents.

The Stories of My Four Friends. Edited by MARGARET ANDREWS ALLEN. Cloth. 100 pages. Fully illustrated. For introduction, 40 cents.

Geographical Plays. Cloth. 140 pages. For introduction, 50 cents.

The "Seven Little Sisters" represents the seven races. The book shows how people live in the various parts of the world, what their manners and customs are, what the products of each section are and how they are interchanged.

"Each and All" continues the story of "Seven Little Sisters," and tells more of the peculiarities of the various races, especially in relation to childhood.

Dame Nature unfolds in "Stories Mother Nature Told" some of her most precious secrets. She tells about the amber, about the dragon-fly and its wonderful history, about water-lilies, how the Indian corn grows, what queer pranks the Frost Giants indulge in, about coral, and starfish, and coal mines, and many other things in which children take delight.

In "Ten Boys" the history of the world is summarized in the stories of Kabla the Aryan boy, Darius the Persian boy, Cleon the Greek boy, Horatius the Roman boy, Wulf the Saxon boy, Gilbert the knight's page, Roger the English boy, Fuller the Puritan boy, Dawson the Yankee boy, and Frank Wilson the boy of 1885.

The "Four Friends" are the four seasons personified. They weave into stories the wonderful workings of nature. Any child who has enjoyed "How the Indian Corn Grows," or "A Peep into One of God's Storehouses," in "Stories Mother Nature Told Her Children," will be glad to read of "Some Frost Flowers," "The North Wind's Birth Gift to the Earth's Youngest Child," which Winter tells, or the spring story of "What Was Heard Under the Ground One April Day."

GINN & COMPANY, Publishers,

Boston.   New York.   Chicago.   San Francisco.
Atlanta.   Dallas.   Columbus.   London.

LONG'S WOOD FOLK SERIES

By William J. Long

WAYS OF WOOD FOLK

Sq. 12mo. Cloth. 205 pages. Illustrated. For introduction, 50 cents.

Fascinating descriptions of the lives and habits of the commoner wood folk, such as the crow, the rabbit, the wild duck. The book is profusely illustrated by Charles Copeland and William Hamilton Gibson.

WILDERNESS WAYS

Sq. 12mo. Cloth. 155 pages. Illustrated. For introduction, 45 cents.

"Wilderness Ways" is written in the same intensely interesting style as its predecessor, "Ways of Wood Folk." The author lets the reader this time into the hidden life of the wilderness, not from books or hearsay, but from years of personal contact with wild things of every description. To read their records is to watch for them by the wilderness rivers or to follow their tracks over the winter barrens.

A delicate personal touch is added to every bird and animal by the use of its Indian name. The author is familiar with the Indian language and character, and when he camps with Simmo the Milicete, and sees things through an Indian's eyes, then he is as close to nature as a man can get. In "Wilderness Ways" we have another record of his observations that one is impelled to read to the last word before he lays it down.

SECRETS OF THE WOODS

12mo. Cloth. 184 pages. Illustrated. For introduction, 50 cents.

This is another vivid chapter in the Wood Folk Series. Deer and squirrel, wood mouse and otter, kingfisher and partridge, with a score of other shy wood-dwellers, appear just as they are in their wilderness homes. The book is a revelation of lives hitherto unknown. The wood mouse that dies of fright in the author's hand, the savage old bull-moose that keeps him overnight in a tree, and the big buck that he follows day after day, — all are full of life and color and intensest interest. He sees everything that passes in the woods, and describes it in clear, crisp Anglo-Saxon that makes the reader see it too and share in his joy of discovery.

GINN & COMPANY Publishers

Boston	New York	Chicago	San Francisco
Atlanta	Dallas	Columbus	London

NATURE STUDY

BOOKS OF SPECIAL VALUE

Stories of Insect Life. (First Series.)

By CLARENCE MOORES WEED, Professor of Zoölogy and Entomology in the New Hampshire College of Agriculture and the Mechanic Arts. 12mo. Boards. 54 pages. Illustrated. For introduction, 25 cents.

The insects treated of in this book are the more interesting common forms of spring and early summer. The story of the life of each is told in a simple way, rendering the book especially desirable for children to read in connection with nature studies of insects.

Stories of Insect Life. (Second Series.)

Summer and Autumn. By MARY E. MURTFELDT and CLARENCE M. WEED. 12mo. Cloth. 72 pages. For introduction, 30 cents.

This book, like its predecessor, aims to give to young pupils an accurate and readable account of the life histories of some common insects. It is designed for use during the autumn months, as the first book was especially intended for use in spring. The paragraphs are short, the language simple, with no more technical words than are absolutely necessary, and each story is compressed into a space that will not weary the child. Throughout the stories the reader is incited to make original observations out of doors. An introductory chapter gives suggestions to the teacher regarding methods of using insects in nature study.

Seed-Travellers.

By CLARENCE M. WEED. 12mo. Boards. 53 pages. Illustrated. For introduction, 25 cents.

This book consists of a series of simple discussions of the more important methods by which seeds are dispersed.

It is designed especially for use during autumn and winter. It is believed that the book will prove of decided value in the practical work of the schoolroom.

GINN & COMPANY, Publishers,

Boston. New York. Chicago. Atlanta. Dallas.